I0055238

Purpose of the Book

[Don't] let anyone convince you that your dream, your vision to be an entrepreneur, is something that you shouldn't do. What often happens is that people who are well meaning, who really care for us, are afraid for us and talk us out of it.

Cathy Hughes, entrepreneur, radio and television personality, and business executive

The book is aimed at giving those that may be interested in entrepreneurship as a career (particularly UBSS local and international students) a feel of what it is "like to be in the driver's seat". This is whether it is in their own organisation or being entrepreneurially minded in someone else's organisation. The book will give readers a feel of everyday Australian business success and help them to earn directly from successful entrepreneurs.

We asked the same 15 questions to 15 "everyday" successful Australian entrepreneurs and then we analysed their answers to see if there are any common themes, and to see if their advice can be of use to business students, or indeed anyone interested in business.

We believe that this book would be particularly helpful for commerce / business students as it will assist them as to whether they wish to be entrepreneurs. Some of the 15 questions were designed to be of direct assistance to this audience.

Naturally it would be good if you could test being an entrepreneur to see if it suits you, but realistically this would be difficult to do. However, with this book at least you can read about entrepreneurs and let all this research help you in deciding whether you want to give entrepreneurship a go.

Figure 1 - Spotting the "potholes in the road"

We seek to help the reader to spot the "potholes in the road" before they hit them and, if they do hit them, be able to mitigate and manage the consequences.

What can we learn from everyday successful Australian entrepreneurs?

All 15 Entrepreneur Interviewees asked the same 15 questions

Front cover top row: *Art Phillips, Andy West, Alan Manly, Greg Whateley, Cyril Jankoff, Daniel Bendel*

Middle row: *Sudhir Warrier, Rahul Daga, Himalee Karunasena, John Engelander, Alice Needham, Cliffy and Philip Chaplin, Ramin (Robert) Roshan*

Front row: *Margaret Harmer, Matija Squire, Jon Tse, Annemarie Manders, Greg Quicke and James Barbour*

Cartoons of contributors (above and on cover) by Jan Harrison

Cyril Jankoff and Daniel Bendel

(With a foreword by Professor Andrew West)

First Published in 2021 by 1visionOT Pty Ltd trading as Smart Questions, Suite 3, 596 North Road, Ormond, VIC 3204, Australia

Web: www.smart-questions.com (including ordering of printed and electronic copies, extended book information and community contributions)

Email: info@smart-questions.com (for customer services, bulk order enquiries, reproduction requests et al)

ISBN 978-1-907453-32-8

SQ-23-203-001-001

Structure of the Book

If something is important enough, or you believe something is important enough, even if you are scared, you will keep going.

Elon Musk, CEO of Tesla Motors and SpaceX

There are entrepreneurs everywhere, all around us, and they are the ones that make things happen. In this book we have tried to work out how everyday entrepreneurs have managed to be, and stay, successful and what we can learn from them.

The structure of the book is:

Part A – The Interviews

We interviewed 15 everyday entrepreneurs and asked them the same 15 questions. You can find each of the interviews here.

Part B – Discussion and analysis

In this Part we discuss and analyse the interviews. We compare interviewee answers and summarise their advice.

Part C – The Theory

In this Part we discuss various theories surrounding entrepreneurship and compare the interviews to the theory.

Part D – References

In the final Part we provide the lists of references, figures etc and an index to enhance your navigation of the book.

Dedication

To our UBSS community who have become like a real family to us and are dedicated to work together to provide real life education for our students from all over the world.

To our own families – Thanks for all your fantastic support.

In some parallel universe we would be working together as architects on the Guggenheim Museum extension.

Figure 2 - Cyril Jankoff and Daniel Bendel in 2021 with 'Business War Stories', their first book

Authors

ASSOCIATE PROFESSOR CYRIL JANKOFF

EdD, MBA, Grad Dip Tax, BBus (Accy), LLB, Dip Contract Mgt, Cert IV TAE, Fellow CFS, Fellow CPA, Fellow AIMWA, Fellow IML, Fellow WorldCC and SRME.

Dr Cyril focuses on business improvement. In his career he practiced as an accountant, solicitor, in-house counsel, business consultant and financial controller and still holds practising certificates as an accountant and solicitor. He also worked as the Australia and Oceania manager for a division of a listed UK multinational and has written two books on improving the management of commercial contracts and another one on finance for contracting and non-finance managers. He frequently facilitates business improvement seminars locally and overseas and has taught continuously at universities on a part-time basis since 1986. Cyril's doctorate was in business improvement, family business and the professional development of those who work in, and advise, these organisations. He is co-author with Daniel Bendel in the UBSS book Business War Stories from the Trenches – Battles relating to starting, operating and ending a business.

DANIEL BENDEL

Bachelor of Business (Distinction), Grad Dip Tax, Fellow CPA and Fellow UBSS CFE.

Daniel commenced his career in the 1970s as a financial accountant in the corporate world, and later went to work in the accounting profession as a tax and business advisory accountant. Early in his career he was asked to join a large family-owned manufacturing company and was there until he retired in late 2019 as part owner, Director and the Company Secretary. Daniel is still involved in the accounting profession and is thus in a rare position to see business from both sides: as a former owner/manager and as a consultant advisor. He is also involved in many other business-related activities and has acted for clients in in a wide variety of activities including restructuring, forensic work, and business change management etc. As well as being a Director he was the Treasurer of a not-for-profit (NFP) organisation for over 10 years. He is co-author with Cyril Jankoff in the UBSS Business War Stories from the Trenches book.

Cyril and Daniel

Daniel and Cyril met while they were studying for their Graduate Diploma in Taxation in 1981 and have since worked together on many business improvement projects, a few of which are included in this book. They would have formed a formal business consulting partnership but were impeded by their inability over the years to agree on whose name should come first. Should the firm name be Jankoff and Bendel or Bendel and Jankoff.

Acknowledgements

The Authors wish to sincerely wish to thank all those assisted in this publication, especially the following (and we apologise in advance if we have forgotten anyone):

Universal Business School of Sydney (UBSS) staff

Adjunct Professor Art Phillips: Director of The Centre For Entrepreneurship, and an entrepreneur extraordinaire himself.

Emeritus Professor Greg Whateley: Deputy Vice Chancellor of Group Colleges of Australia, the parent company of the Universal Business School of Sydney (UBSS).

Professor Andrew West: UBSS Dean.

Interviewees

The Authors also wish to sincerely thank all the Interviewees for their contributions, their advice, their time and their photos without which this book would be significantly smaller.

Cartoons

The Authors also gratefully acknowledge the cartoons of *Jan Harrison* and *Sharon Madder.*

Cover editing and creative work

Rahul Daga of Snap Printing, Darlinghurst, Sydney.

Formatting, layout and printing

Stephen Parker of Smart Questions

Formatting of the Interviewees on the UBSS website

Doris Leung and *Renee Stabile* of CampusQ.

Table of Contents

SECTION B

SECTION C

SECTION D

Foreword

Universal Business School Sydney's (UBSS) motto is to "launch the careers of tomorrow's entrepreneurs by delivering world-class Business, Accounting and MBA programs through flexible study options that give students the greatest advantage possible." What better way to learn how to launch an entrepreneurial career than learning from those who have succeeded in the past.

Once again, we are honoured to have Associate Professor Cyril Jankoff and his long-term business partner Daniel Bendel to develop, facilitate and compile a series of interviews with entrepreneurs from a wide range backgrounds and endeavours to attain lifelong achievements.

After the success of the first book 'Business War Stories – Battles relating to starting, operating and ending a business', which was based on their own experiences in business, Cyril and Danny were looking to build on their many contributions to the Centre for Entrepreneurship. From the idea to broaden the scope of what it is to be an entrepreneur and the life of an entrepreneur, came their second book 'What Can We Learn From Everyday Successful Entrepreneurs'.

The concept of asking the same 15 questions of the 15 entrepreneur interviewees was conceived by Cyril and Danny. It is an innovative way to gather insights into an entrepreneur's life, highlighting the twisted and rocky path that is an entrepreneur's journey. The format provides the inspiring entrepreneur's stories through the interviews in Part A, the insights of discussion in Part B and the educational linkage with the entrepreneurial theories in Part C.

As the Dean of UBSS, I wish to give my heartfelt thanks to Cyril and Daniel in bringing this book to fruition. I hope you enjoy this book with the many inspiring stories from everyday Australian entrepreneurs.

Professor Andrew West

Dean, Universal Business School Sydney

Preface

An entrepreneur is a person who sets up a business or businesses, taking on financial risks in the hope of profit.

Alan Manly

Definition

One definition of an entrepreneur is an individual who creates a new business, bearing most of the risks and enjoying most of the rewards. The entrepreneur is commonly seen as an innovator, a source of new ideas, goods, services, and business/or procedures (Investopedia, 2021a).

Another similar, but lengthier, definition is that an entrepreneur is (1) An innovator or developer who recognises and seizes opportunities; converts these opportunities into workable/ marketable ideas; adds value through time, effort, money or skills; assumes the risks of the competitive marketplace to implement these ideas; and realises the rewards from these efforts. (2) An individual who organises and manages labour, capital, and natural resources to produce goods and services to earn a profit, but who also runs the risk of failure (Frederick, 2018).

However, a short and easy to remember definition is Alan Manly's 2021 definition: "a person who sets up a business or businesses, taking on financial risks in the hope of profit". Due to its conciseness, we will use this definition in this book.

"Everyday" and successful entrepreneurs

We all hear of very successful business entrepreneurs such as Bill Gates, Andrew Forrest, Richard Branson, etc. Are they any different to the "everyday" successful entrepreneur? Possibly yes, and possibly no. Perhaps they were simply at the right place at the right time to transform a small business into a very large business, or perhaps they do have something special. Either way, the average business student may not get to be the next Mike Cannon-Brookes (Atlassian), but they can realistically aspire to the achievements made by any of the people in the case studies in this book.

What makes people decide on becoming an entrepreneur?

Often it just takes one life-changing moment that creates the spark, "the sliding door moment". In the interviews we can see a number of life changing moments occurring, and they include John Engelander (Interview 4) cleaning toilets, Margaret Harmer (Interview 9) having a tragic car accident and Greg Quicke (Interview 14) just looking up at the stars.

Life changing moments

We are sure that everyone reading this will also have had their own life changing moments. As is often said "it is not the moment itself but how we react and cope with the event that determines the outcomes".

Focus of the book

This book is not focused on the theoretical aspects of entrepreneurship, but on the practical, that is what our everyday entrepreneurs have faced in real life. In order to obtain a more robust view of the interviews we asked each interviewee the same questions about their backgrounds before starting on the business questions.

Figure 3 - What was your life-changing moment that motivated you to start your own business? What might it be?

Notes for the facilitator

If this book is used in an education setting or business course training, the facilitator may wish to discuss how the interviews relate to entrepreneurial theory. The Authors note that by the end of the book readers should at least be able to spell "entrepreneur"!

Improvements, comments etc

If you wish to suggest an improvement to the content or make a comment, then please contact: Cyril Jankoff at *Cyril.Jankoff@ubss.edu.au*

Part A:

What Can We Learn from Everyday Successful Australian Entrepreneurs?

Sudhir Warrier

From fruit and vegies to Cruise ships. From migrant to founder of a successful cruise ship business on Sydney Harbour.

INTRODUCTION

Key points from the interview

- Look at the commerciality of your decisions.
- Importance of reviewing cash flow and profit and loss figures as regularly as possible.
- Always select the best person for the job.
- The benefit of flexibility and having some good connections.
- In following through actions, plans, or ideas until you have done everything possible.
- Keep a balanced approach to risk.
- His advice to other Indians is that do not come to Australia just to make money. Australia is a great place to live well.

Sudhir Warrier (He is known to all as "Warrier")

Combining Malayali (native speakers of Malayalam, originating from the Indian state of Kerala) pragmatism with Australian entrepreneurship and risk-taking.

Further information

- *https://www.sydneyshowboats.com.au/*
- *https://www.sydneyshowboats.com.au/more-info/about-us*

Category

Traditional Entrepreneur: Traditional business entrepreneurs usually gain experience working in the Industry, and then make the move to running their own business either by taking over an existing business or buying or setting up a new one. They bring a wealth of strong relationships with employees, clients and suppliers, and their experience in all aspects of the operations of the business.

I. KEY DATES

- Sudhir Warrier grew up in India.
- In 1985 he completed a Diploma in Hotel Management in Mumbai. He then worked as a catering manager on oil and gas platforms in the Bombay High offshore oilfield.
- Between 1987 and 1990 Warrier ran a wholesale vegetable business in his hometown (Kochi, Kerala, India).
- In 1990 he sold the vegetable business and moved to Sydney as a student. Like many other students, to fund his course fees, the 26-year-old Sudhir started working as a waiter in a restaurant for Sydney Showboats (Blueline Cruises that he later bought).
- In 1994, Sydney Showboat 2 was added to the field, and Warrier was promoted as operations manager.

- In 1996 he left Blueline cruises for 2 years and worked for amalgamated holdings as General Manager of Matilda Cruises.
- In 1998 Warrier was hired back by Blueline Cruises as CEO.
- In 2005 he acquired the entire business with the help of debt funding from the Bank.
- In 2012 he formed the Australian Cruise Group in which he is now the Chief Executive Officer.
- Over the years, Warrier's company acquired more vessels including in 2016 a boutique glass boat with a 360-degree view.
- Always looking at strategy, he acquired Flagship in 2018, Sydney's original charter booking agency.
- His cruise company is now a large SME (small medium-sized enterprise).
- Warrier has kept his connection with India alive by keeping up to date with current affairs, cricket and visiting family as often as he can.

II. GETTING TO KNOW THE PERSON

1. What is success?

Warrier sees success in business terms. He feels that it is a little like a scoreboard: if he accumulates more wins than losses then that is success. Even a small margin, for example, 20% of wins over losses is acceptable. The profit and loss statement is another indicator of success. He does not look at personal life the same way and keeps that separate.

2. What is your favourite TV show, movie or book and why?

Warrier enjoys the "Bollywood" style movies, particularly from Southern India for relaxation. He does not watch much television.

3. What are your hobbies and/or Interests?

Warrier loves cricket, playing and watching. He also plays social badminton with a regular group.

III. TIPS

4. How did you get through your worst times?

The 2002-2004 Severe Acute Respiratory Syndrome (SARS) was a viral respiratory disease and had some effect on cruising in 2003, but it did not hit him hard as he purchased the business in 2005. However, 18 months after he purchased the business the Global Financial Crisis (GFC) hit the world. Warrier's business, was hit very hard as he had to service the debt. Since the GFC the business has done well until the 2020 Covid-19 pandemic hit. This will be discussed in Section V, below.

5. What keeps you awake at night?

Not much keeps him awake at night. Warrier can switch off after working hours. He thinks his daily routines help, discussed in the next question immediately below. Other things that help are light entertainment such as cricket or Bollywood movies.

6. What are your typical daily routines?

Warrier has a predictable routine and works from 8 am to 8 pm. He gets to sleep around 11 pm, and up at about 6 am. His routines include:

- In the morning he has a coffee, reads the news and goes for early morning walks, and often walks to work across the Sydney Harbour Bridge.
- His assistant arrives at 9 am.
- He usually schedules any meetings after lunch so that urgent matters can be dealt with early.
- He has 2 meetings per week, sales and operations meetings.

- Warrier says he prefers little bureaucracy and feels the culture of the organisation is very important and everyone knows to limit internal emails to around 20, and to only copy in someone (cc) if it is vital to do so.
- He encourages people to talk and communicate.
- They often meet at the office "water cooler", which is a large bench under a tree nearby their offices. This is a good place to stop and think.

7. What advice would you give yourself starting out?

Warrier advises young people starting off to be careful about blindly following personal passions and they need to look at the commerciality of their decisions. He suggested that the main problem in starting out is often working capital, that is having adequate cash as and when required. Accountants call this having adequate cash flow. He recognises the importance of reviewing cash flow and profit and loss figures as regularly as possible. He gives further advice that one needs to be very careful about hiring anyone you know. Always select the best person for the job.

IV. BUSINESS CASE EXAMPLES

8. Provide a case you managed well and why?

Figure 4 - Warrier and his two cruise ships: Clearview on the left and Sydney Showboats on the right

The first example occurred on New Year's Eve 2019 when he had 2500 passengers wanting to take one of his tours, but he only had 1300 available seats. He managed to charter extra boats to cater for the demand. What is the lesson to be learnt? He says flexibility and the benefit of having some good connections.

The second example occurred after the Ocean Spirit disaster described in Question 10, below. This is where Warrier re-focused on his key strength, the Sydney Harbour cruise market. After 18 months an opportunity to buy a boutique glass boat arose. With mainly "gut feel" he purchased the boat, and the acquisition has been so successful that within a short period he purchased a second boat and launched the business as "Clearview Cruises". It is now the top cruise operator in Sydney. The lesson? Be flexible and open to opportunities.

9. Provide a case that did not go well and why?

Warrier's business is seasonal being busy during the October to March warmer months. To even up his business he looked to buy a business that is busy in the alternative season, that is in July and August. Warrier found a business that fitted this strategy in 2011, when Warrier purchased the Ocean Spirit business in Cairns.

He commissioned several expert reports and did a careful due diligence on the new business. However, despite all this, the business did not do well and after 2 years they had to sell it.

The problems were the twin issues of being overconfident about their business model and underestimating the local competition. Warrier's Sydney business was very strong with good systems and had a good relationship with the local booking agents. However, this was not the case in Cairns, northern Queensland. The local Cairns agent network operators did not want to support an "outsider" and did not promote his business but did promote his competition. In summary, Warrier analysed the business itself but failed to look at the potential threats from taking over a local business with its own politics.

How could he have avoided the problem? Assuming he still would have gone ahead with buying the business, Warrier says he would have restructured the business into a different model, that is he would have:

- operated a more of a cut down ("Jetstar" model), that is it could have been more cost effective; and

- kept fixed costs down (no expensive offices, photocopier leases etc).

Clearly a combination of tough business conditions and being locked into high costs cost the business dearly. Perhaps if the fixed costs were lower the business may have been able to slowly rebuild after the initial difficulties with the local agents.

10. What conclusions can be drawn by comparing these cases?

Warrier has learnt the importance of looking at what can go wrong when evaluating business opportunities. He sees external "threats", which are these events that occur outside your control, as the most important element of the well-known SWOT (Strengths, Weaknesses, Opportunities and Threats) system of business evaluation.

The strengths and weaknesses relate to the internal environment, being an environment that you have control over. The opportunities and threats relate to the external environment, the environment which you have no control over. Examples include COVID-19, interest rates, economic conditions and competition.

11. What cultural issues did you experience? How were they overcome? How is Australia different? Were these cases affected by cultural issues?

Warrier says none of his business ventures have been affected by cross cultural issues.

> **Authors' note:** Perhaps his understanding of, and sensitivity towards, the difference between Australian and Indian work cultures has meant that there are no resulting problems of significance.

Warrier said that he has offices in India and Australia and that there are differences in the way his Indian and Australian staff work.

Australians are more structured. For example, they often have set routines of, say always having a family meal at 6.30pm. Australian culture sees one's work and private lives as separate and distinct. By contrast Indian culture is that these areas merge, and their work is much more fluid. One night an employee may work to 6 pm but on a regular basis they may work far longer. In India working hours are much more flexible.

Warrier takes these differences into account when he manages his Indian and Australian staff. His Indian employees are often more flexible and often prepared to work extra hours to get the job done. In contrast he finds that Australians are focused on getting the job done in the hours available thus they can be more efficient.

Asian culture tends to have a more structured "class orientation" compared to Australia. Age and Titles are more significant in Asia. Australia is much more egalitarian which has some positives and negatives in terms of managing employees and his approach is modified when managing in Australia. For example, he would rarely ask an Australian employee for something after 7 pm.

Gender has not been a big issue for them. Hospitality and Tourism have a high female participation rate which leads to a positive culture. The operational area (ship operations) is mainly male, but he has not faced any gender problems.

Many of his ship operational staff (captains) are long standing, some in the business for over 20 years. One of the existing effects of COVID-19 is that because of Government support it has become difficult to recruit waiters. He said that it will be interesting when Government support reduces at the end of March 2021.

V. VOLATILITY (FOR EXAMPLE COVID)

12. How has the virus affected your business?

In 2020 Covid-19 pandemic, with operations closed for 6 months. Later outbreaks mean that he missed the lucrative Boxing Day (2020), New Year's Eve (2020) and Australia Day (2021) markets. On New Year's Eve 2020 his business had 150 bookings, which was a 94% reduction on the previous year due to COVID-19. This shows that external factors can affect any business no matter how well run. Warrier's business was effectively closed for 6 months. He is confident that business will improve but sees 2021 and even 2022 still being impacted and a full return to normal business in 2023. He said that the business had to stand down 120 staff but recognises the assistance of Jobkeeper and other subsidies to keep the business going.

13. What lasting impact do you think it will have on your business?

Warrier sees COVID-19 as a wake-up call. He feels he could have been better prepared to deal with the pandemic. He thinks businesses need to review their operations and resources regularly and closely. His business has a high labour input cost in its operating cost structure, and thus the business needs to carefully manage its labour.

Although the business was not operating during the COVID-19 lockdown, key staff were still working hard on the firm's marketing strategies and planning for the future.

Previously 75% passengers were international passengers, but in early 2021 they are at 100% local passengers. In early 2021 the business is running cruises 6 to 8 cruises per week, while in the pre-COVID-19 world it was 55 cruises per week.

There is an increased amount of bureaucracy in dealing with the complex protocols relating to COVID-19 safety, and this has been reasonably challenging. Warrier has found generally the level of bureaucracy in his business is acceptable.

Warrier stated that he was in the process of evaluating a $30 million business purchase just before COVID-19 hit. He did not proceed and feels that he has "dodged a bullet".

14. What have you learned from it that you will now implement in your business?

COVID-19 has brought him back to the drawing board and is working hard to re-evaluate his business to cope with these difficult times. He watches his profit and loss statement very closely and does so almost daily. He also focuses on the trading profit rather than net profit after fixed costs. This is so that he can make quick decisions on his controllable area of costs which exclude fixed costs.

Australia is a relaxed place to live. He has found working hard can pay off well in Australia and is very appreciative of his Australian home. Warrier concentrates on two areas:

- Need to be connected to his staff (not least because labour costs are very high); and
- Need to watch the product being delivered.

As for the secret of success Warrier believes:

- In following through actions, plans, or ideas until you have done everything possible.
- He has a very balanced approach to risk.
- His advice to other Indians is that do not come to Australia just to make money. Australia is a place to live well.

VI. FAMILY BUSINESS

15. Are you in a family business and from your experience what do you think are the advantages and disadvantages of family working in the business?

No. *"To be honest, I see no advantages for family working in the business unless there are 2 specific reasons.*

1. *They have the best skills for a particular role.*
2. *They are being groomed to take over the business.*

From my experience, multiple family members (especially husband and wife) working together is rarely a good model. I hear staff complaining about this scenario in many other businesses.

When it comes to me, I believe in a committee of 1 – just me.

My family members are not directors either, I make all of the decisions so that the senior management has clear direction, rather than mixed messaging, especially when it comes to marketing and product delivery"

FUN FACTS ON: ...

Steam-powered boats

When told of Robert Fulton's steamboat in the early 1800s Napoleon Bonaparte didn't have the time to listen to such nonsense: *"How, sir, would you make a ship sail against the wind and currents by lighting a bonfire under deck?"* According to Sam USACE Army (2021) the first successful steamboat was the Clermont, which was built by American inventor Robert Fulton in 1807.

Flight

Flight by machines heavier than air is unpractical and insignificant, if not utterly impossible.

Simon Newcomb, Canadian American astronomer and mathematician, 18 months before the Wright Brothers' flight at Kittyhawk

Personal Helicopters

In 1951, Popular Mechanics claimed that we would all have our own personal helicopters by 2020.

Rail

Rail Travel at high speed is not possible because passengers, unable to breathe would die of asphyxia

De. Dionysys Larder, professor of Natural Philosophy & Astronomy, University College London. 1800

Cars

Nothing has come along that can beat the horse and buggy (Circa 1900-1910)

Chauncey DePew, president of the New York Central Railroad, warning his nephew against investing in Henry Ford's new company

The horse is here to stay, but the automobile is only a novelty, a fad (Circa 1900-1910)

The President of the Michigan Savings Bank advising Henry Ford's lawyer not to invest in the Ford Motor company.

Rahul Daga

From migrant to owner of two profitable Snap printing franchises.

INTRODUCTION

Key points from the interview

- Rahul observes the mantra: listen, observe and act.
- In times of failure, keep trying as every situation is different
- It was the networking with other students that he has found the most valuable and would emphasise to prospective students as one key benefit of studying with people.
- He advises that it is important to support staff and give them the creative freedom to add value to the business, and they can often surprise you with their problem-solving creativity.

Rahul Daga

Combining a solid foundation of technical skills and family support to enable an entrepreneurial outlook.

Rahul had a solid technical training and working background in India and the UK. He migrated to Australia initially working in sales for a Snap printing franchise.

This experience combined with his technical background eventually culminated in him owning and operating his own Snap printing franchises

Further information

- *https://www.snap.com.au/snap-darlinghurst.html*

Category

Technical entrepreneur. A technical entrepreneur uses technology as a base to add other management skills including sales and marketing to build a business.

I. KEY DATES

- Rahul was raised in Solapur and Mumbai, India.
- He has been with his Dimple, now his wife since he was 18. He considers her his biggest support.
- 1987-1990: Diploma in Mechanical Engineering, India.
- 1990-1993: Diploma in Printing Technology, India.
- 1994-1995: Diploma in Lithography, at Westheart College, Watford, UK
- 1995-1999: Worked in India as a production manager.
- 1999-2004: Production Manager in Dubai printing industry
- 2004: Migrated to Australia 2004 and first job with Snap Franchising as a sales consultant.
- 2004-2006:
  - Worked with Snap as a sales consultant for 2 franchises.
  - Formed long term relationship with CEO and marketing heads of Snap Franchising office who offered Rahul an opportunity in a pilot program of a 'mobile franchise' of Snap Printing in 2011.

- 2006-2011: Further experience gained in business development in the industry.
- Jun 2011: Signed agreement with Snap Franchise to commence a mobile franchise for a new territory, which had no previous franchise and did not have any existing clients.
- Sept 2011: A large client from previous employment position approached Rahul to take over their print and marketing requirements as they were more comfortable to deal with him.
- 2011-2014: He door knocked every business in the territory to introduce Snap's services.
- March 2017: He bought Snap Kingsgrove, a second Snap Printing franchise to support his first franchise in Darlinghurst with a production facility and be able to control delivery times and quality of products. Snap Darlinghurst earns double the revenue of Snap Kingsgrove. The combined revenue of both franchises reached one million dollars in June 2019.

II. GETTING TO KNOW THE PERSON

1. What is success?

Rahul sees obtaining results from hard work as success, particularly if it is his clients that are happy and satisfied. It means his hard work has paid off and is recognised. For example, from 2009 he managed to prove himself a reliable supplier at a reasonable price to the Universal Business School of Sydney (UBSS), the publisher of this book. This makes him feel successful.

2. What is your favourite TV show, movie or book and why?

He said that he does not have much time for TV, but he does watch occasional movies, reads books, and more recently he listens to audio books. His favourite book is *Bhagavad Gita*, the Hindu scripture that is considered to be the one of the main holy scriptures for Hinduism. He sees it as India's Bible and to him is a philosophy of life.

3. What are your hobbies and/or Interests?

Rahul likes watching and playing sport, particularly swimming. He represented his school at State level and pre-COVID-19 he was swimming several times per week. He used to teach swimming. To release work pressure, Rahul goes for bush walking, cooks and sometimes also plays the bamboo flute. He uses YouTube for cooking tips.

III. TIPS

4. How did you get through your worst times?

Rahul landed in Australia with production and technical skills. He had a family to support so he had to find work. However, he found the Australian market saturated with people with similar skills and thus he could not find work. On top of that, as he was used to the British accent in India, he had difficulty understanding the Australian accent and had to ask people to repeat themselves.

Faced with all these difficulties and not wanting to go back to India he had to re-invent himself. As he was not afraid of trying something different, he decided to use his knowledge of the printing industry to move into the business development / sales / marketing sides of printing. With his wife, Dimple, and family support, he decided to go into this side of the printing industry.

From 2004 to 2011 he worked for others. His family was a great source of support during these times. Rahul also kept strong mentally and physically and kept working hard. He emphasises perseverance and never give up attitude. Rahul observes the mantra: listen, observe and act. In times of failure, keep trying as every situation is different.

His relatives were successful. His father, a hard worker, who was a Chartered Accountant, is 73 and is very active and was, and is, a great mentor and inspiration for him. Rahul's father-in-law started out as precious stone grinder at the age of 10 and at 77 was

Mumbai's biggest precious stone dealer and was Rahul's biggest inspiration. He died late last year.

5. What keeps you awake at night?

Nothing, as Rahul sleeps well at night. His wife often asks him why he sleeps so well? He responds that he avoids dwelling on issues. He also feels that he sleeps well due to his regular exercise and particularly his daily yoga. Furthermore, Rahul takes care to thoroughly finish his tasks for the day so that he can start the next day fresh and can sleep peacefully.

6. What are your typical daily routines?

Rahul likes to follow the "Early to bed and early to rise". In the mornings he meditates, exercises, has a good breakfast and leaves for the office early. At work he organises his day as follows: phone calls early, appointments with clients mid-morning and site visits in the afternoon.

7. What advice would you give yourself starting out?

He purchased his first franchise in 2011 and he has been pleasantly surprised by how people were willing to help him. Rahul's advice is not to be afraid to ask people.

Authors' note: Just like you should not be afraid to ask for directions if you are lost.

Rahul suggests contacting successful people in your field to see how they have done it and ask them for some mentoring and some tips.

He advises that the future of the printing industry is changing and becoming more personalised and more work on demand. It is certainly more complex than 10 to 15 years ago. He found that 3D printing is a slow growth business and has its own specific needs.

His printing business includes a wide variety of products in addition to specialised business cards, and includes packaging, labelling, signage and a variety of marketing branding applications.

He advised that it took him seven and a half years to complete an MBA (a Master of Business Administration) degree, but it was the networking with other students that he has found the most valuable and would emphasise to prospective students this as a key benefit of an MBA. Studying while working and with a family requires perseverance and again was thankful for his family support.

He feels that life is a matter of choice, live well, never stop learning, learn from experts in the field. He considers that one should not be swayed by adverse conditions, and one should keep doing one's job with integrity, keep sowing the seeds for future success. He feels that fruits will come so there is a necessity to be patient. He reminded the authors of the saying that 'Rome wasn't built in a day!'

IV. BUSINESS CASE EXAMPLES

8. Provide a case you managed well and why?

One of Rahul's clients received a last-minute update from its client Tennis Australia which wanted 100% recyclable racquet tags for the Australian Open and wanted them as soon as possible. A deliverable was that the tag needed to be strong, light and flexible at the same time.

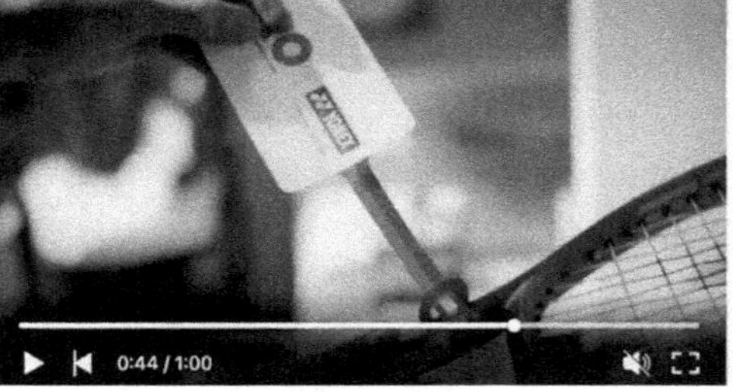

Figure 5 - The 100% recyclable racquet tags for the Australian Open

Rahul had to research various types of stocks as it was a very challenging requirement. Finally, with his contacts he found a synthetic stock which was also recyclable. This was then printed from a specially die and cut to a shape which worked perfectly for tagging the racquet. To the right is a picture of the tag in the video being promoted by Yonex Australia, a leader in tennis equipment. Here is the link to the video/post: *https://www.linkedin.com/in/dagarahul/detail/recent-activity/*. This solution proved successful as it met his client's technical and budgetary requirements.

Rahul feels that this was a good example of a team effort to think creatively to provide a solution to the client. He advises that it is important to support staff and give them the creative freedom to add value to the business, and they can often surprise you with their problem-solving creativity.

9. Provide a case that did not go well and why?

In 2017 when he purchased his second franchise there were staff difficulties and the existing employees decided to leave and join the departing franchise holder. He found running two franchises quite difficult but his wife, Dimple proved to be invaluable. The arrangement now is that for the two franchises she manages the customer services side whilst he manages the technical side.

The reason for buying second franchise was to streamline increasing demand and meet client timelines. However suddenly he found all his plans came undone as the production facility did not have a production manager. He temporarily went back to previous arrangements where he had outsourced their production of goods to keep clients happy. This was resolved once his staffing issues was fixed.

10. What conclusions can be drawn by comparing these cases?

Rahul says *"A Plan B or even a Plan C is required in business situations. In any situation, the customer should be the priority and then profitability."*

11. What cultural issues did you experience? How were they overcome? How is Australia different? Were these cases affected by cultural issues?

Rahul has never had a bad experience in Australia in relation to cultural issues. The Australian accent was a challenge at the beginning. In addition, it took some time before he could understand the slang. Rahul says none of the cases had any cultural issues.

V. VOLATILITY (FOR EXAMPLE COVID)

12. How has the virus affected your business?

A major part of Rahul's revenue is from the event and training industry. These were severely affected by COVID-19 as there was little or no face-to-face training or gatherings. As a majority of industries and offices were initially directed to work from home the demand for printing diminished overnight. This severely affected the industry. His business revenue dropped 60% as a result. Rahul says, "As everyone knows, many businesses moved their services online, for example fitness classes were being conducted on Zoom and also many events became hybrid so there were only limited face-to-face attendees".

It was interesting that during the pandemic there was a 40% increase in new business registrations with ASIC as more people are starting their own businesses.

13. What lasting impact do you think it will have on your business?

We are seeing businesses keen to go back to live events and training, citing the reduced return on investment (ROI) with online events, and the lack of participant engagement. At the same time, health restrictions, keeping a safe distance and hygiene requirements will continue for near future. This will impact on costs, so there could be continuing squeezes on prices throughout the supply chain.

Rahul is now more optimistic and confident that Events will come back strongly. The training side of his business may in the future have a more hybrid style of delivery, that is combining online and face to face delivery. Rahul said that he is happy that his machines are busy and that things are looking positive for the future.

14. What have you learned from it that you will now implement in your business?

Businesses will have to reinvent ways to make things more personal or engaging with their audience to be more successful. It will also need to diversify in different products so that next impact of any catastrophic event does not impact the businesses severely. He has also learnt the need to diversify his client base. Had he had business clients in industries other than training and education then he feels that the impact may have been less severe.

Rahul said he also needs to be careful about incurring large expenses. They are now looking at doing more sharing of resources with other Snap franchisees, particularly with expensive equipment. He said that technology changes so quickly that the sharing of risk through sharing equipment makes financial sense. He is also seeing some operators cutting prices to obtain business. He feels that this is not a sustainable model and is creating a problem for everyone, and that there may be a correction in the Industry as a result.

VI. FAMILY BUSINESS

15. Are you in a family business and from your experience what do you think are the advantages and disadvantages of family working in the business?

Rahul thinks his business is a family business as he and Dimple both work together, but in different capacities.

Rahul advises that everyone is different, and it is important to allow for everyone's individual personalities and skills. It is important to treat the workplace for business only and if family members are working in different areas of the business there is less potential for conflict. The problem often arises when one family member reports directly to another and thus it is usually better to keep functional reporting separate.

Rahul says "Working with family members can be beneficial to all members if done carefully. It has obvious advantages like trust, sharing of responsibilities and also flexibility regarding time and work". If there is unclear communication between family members, then there is a possibility for conflict, and this can affect the business. This in turn can affect their personal relationship, particularly if they live together. Patience and good communication are extremely important to make these work effectively.

Authors' note: Rahul's franchises supply UBSS with its printing needs.

Figure 6 – Rahul's Workhorse

FUN FACTS ON: ...

The printing press is either the greatest blessing or the greatest curse of modern times, sometimes one forgets which it is.

E.F Schumacher

If all printers were determined not to print anything till, they were sure it would offend nobody, there would be very little printed.

Benjamin Franklin

Some common phrases that come from the printing industry:

- **Making a Good Impression**: This is essential advice for job interviews and first dates, making a good impression wasn't always defined as crucial advice to guarantee others have a good opinion of you. Back in the day, the idiom was an instruction to printers to ensure the printing plates and blocks made a good impression on the paper to let the ink soak in.
- **Cliché**: Stolen from our French friends. Cliché originally referred to the solid plate of type metal which was made from a cast. This fixed printing cast is where we find the source of the recent meaning in the English Language, of a fixed idea or phrase which hasn't changed overtime until it is completely overused and unoriginal.
- **A Dab Hand**: Printers used a 'dab' to apply ink onto the letter blocks until they were ready to be applied. Whoever had the job to make sure there was even coverage of the letters with the mushroom shaped instrument was thus graced the title of 'dab hand', hence our common use of someone skilled at a certain ability

Source: Instantprint (2021).

Himalee Karunasena

From a migrant to founding and operating various businesses while being an employee.

INTRODUCTION

Key points from the interview

- Be careful when going into a new area. Australia has so many opportunities, but it is advisable to study the area you are interested in.
- Taking a break from a problem often allows the mind to relax and let the subconscious do the work.
- Importance of 'local knowledge' while taking business risks.
- Before buying a business there is a big advantage in working in a similar one first for a while to pick up the nuances. This is especially valid in the more regulated type of businesses.
- In this land of opportunities anyone can achieve success if they are confident and prepared to take some risk.

Himalee Karunasena

A natural Entrepreneur for both her family and for the community.

Himalee migrated to Australia from Sri Lanka and was quite shy and protected within her community and in an arranged marriage. Slowly whilst working as an Accountant she developed a lot of self-confidence to the point of establishing several successful businesses.

Category

Part time entrepreneur. Student to employee where she has remained but has been actively involved in family entrepreneurship outside her steady employment (The balance small business, 2021). Himalee herself may be part time but each of her businesses has full time staff including family members.

I. KEY DATES

- Himalee migrated to Australia in 1988 when she was in her early twenties. She had her accounting qualifications but was lacking experience in general business.
- She was soon able to obtain an accounting position in a medium size manufacturing company.
- Himalee continued to study to improve her qualifications and became heavily involved in community activities and volunteering for a large array of professional and social causes (see list in Question 3, below).
- She married Vijaya, a Civil Engineer and had her wedding in Sri Lanka in 1992.
- She is always keen to look out for opportunities.
- Started Taprobane Books and Gifts to import books on Buddhism from Sri Lanka to the first ever Buddhist convention held in Australia in 2002.
- Her first major opportunity came when she purchased a petrol station business with her brother and sister-in-law in 2004.
- In 2008 she bought the petrol station's freehold property.

- From 2010, she saw an opportunity for Taprobane Books and Gifts to supply books and other items to refugee camps under Australian Government control.
- In 2013 she purchased a local post office in partnership with her sister and brother-in-law, with each family owning 50% of the business.
- Himalee went part time with her employment with the manufacturing company to concentrate on her business activities and to complete her registration as a Tax Agent. She has pursued this to provide long-term retirement income.
- She investigated purchasing a business providing tax return lodgement type services but when she did her due diligence, she found out that the business was not run properly. As a result, she did not proceed with the purchase. This matter is discussed in more detail in Case 1 in Item 10.
- Himalee has continually been reinvesting her income into a property portfolio.
- Her husband manages the IT needs of the various businesses.

II. GETTING TO KNOW THE PERSON

1. What is success?

Himalee sees success as achieving a number of things which are more or less in the following order:

- Happy family life.
- Financial independence, for both during the main part of her life and for the retirement phase.
- Ability to help people less fortunate than herself.
- Achieving work fulfilment.

2. What is your favourite TV show, movie or book and why?

Himalee likes classic musicals, her favourite being the *'Sound of Music'*. She likes the philosophy in the movie. She admits to watching some *NCIS* on TV. In addition, Himalee watches the occasional Sri Lankan movie in Sinhalese, the main Sri Lankan language.

3. What are your hobbies and/or Interests?

Himalee has many hobbies and interests:

- Travelling, sightseeing, family outings and fine dining. She has been to many places including New Zealand, USA, Canada, Mexico, Thailand, India, Sri Lanka, Singapore, Malaysia, Myanmar and Maldives. She said that on her to do list is Europe, Japan, Egypt, Vietnam, partake in an African safari and relax on an Alaskan cruise.
- Movies, stage shows, musical events and dinner dances.
- Enjoyed broadcasting on SBS radio and 3ZZZ radio Sinhala programs and producing children's TV programs for Sri Lanka Morning Show on Channel 31 on Sundays.
- Supervisor, CPA Program – employed by Pearson Education. Marked candidate responses for Ethics and Governance since 2000. Received Certificate of Acknowledgement for participation and contribution to 25 marking weekends of CPA Program.
- Board member and the Treasurer of School Council of the Victorian School of Languages since 2004.
- Board member and the Treasurer of VICSEG (Victorian Cooperative on Children's Services for Ethnic Groups) New Futures since 2016. This is an incorporated not for profit, community organisation.
- Board Member and the Treasurer of Hume Whittlesea Local Learning and Employment Network (HWLLEN) since 2019. It is a not-for-profit membership-based organisation that works at the strategic level to assist young people to complete Year 12, or its equivalent, and improve transition outcomes for them.

- A founding governor and the treasurer of the Migraine Foundation Australia since 2019.
- Honorary treasurer for two community organisations and honorary auditor for 8 community organisations.
- A pioneer in Sinhala Language teaching in northern suburbs for over 30 years.
- Chairperson of the Sri Lankan Ladies Group of Whittlesea since 2015.
- Vice President of Foundation of Mindfulness Australia since 2018.
- Contested for North East Ward of the City of Whittlesea at 2012 Council Elections but was not successful.
- Was a member of the Sustainability Advisory Committee and Litter Prevention Taskforce of the Whittlesea Council.
- Treasurer of the Northern Melbourne Sri Lankan Seniors Club since its inception in 2008 and enjoys providing volunteer services to senior Citizens.
- Certificate of Appreciation in recognition of voluntary service to the community in 2001 International Year of Volunteers from the State Government.
- 'Radio Presenter (Female) of the year 2006' award presented by Serendib News Awards at Crown Palladium in Melbourne.
- Certificate of Appreciation for the contribution to 2009 SBS Radio and Red Cross Bushfire Appeal, from SBS Radio.
- 'Recognition of Excellence Service' award from Victorian School of Languages (VSL) – 2011.
- 'Female Volunteer - 2014 Business & Community Award' presented by Serendib News Awards at The Grand on Princes in Mulgrave.
- Certificate of Congratulations for Volunteer Services to the Community - April 2021

Authors' note:

1. One of the Authors has a personal recollection of Himalee's desire to help communities. In around 1996 she was working as an employee accountant for a large manufacturing company. She heard that a radio station was promoting a competition with the prize being a private concert for the winner's employer by a popular local music band known as "Bachelor Girl". She quickly entered the competition and won the prize. She approached the manufacturing company, which was very conservative and initially very reticent. However, she managed to persuade senior management (with help from the author) to host the pop group. It was a fantastic day and a huge morale boost to the staff.
2. How does she have the time?

III. TIPS

4. How did you get through your worst times?

As a keen follower of Buddhism Himalee applies its philosophy and wisdom to overcome challenging and difficult situations. Her family support also helps a great deal when she needs extra support.

5. What keeps you awake at night?

Himalee finds that she can separate business issues from personal matters and is able to 'switch off' to give herself some space. Interestingly she often wakes up with the solution to a technical business problem she has been struggling with. She feels that taking a break from a problem often allows her mind to relax and let the subconscious do the work. She feels that practising Buddhism and meditation assists her.

6. What are your typical daily routines?

Himalee often takes a walk in the afternoon. She normally wakes at 6 am and goes to bed at 11 pm. She has volunteered to organise devotees to offer daily lunch for monks in a Buddhist Monastery. She checks the Monastery's website every morning for requests from devotees to offer lunch and allocate dates for them. She then has a system including:

- checking all her banking balances and transactions.

Authors' note: An excellent way of picking any fraud early

- checking Facebook for 5-10 minutes for any special social events
- checking her emails for any business issues
- clearing any action items and putting emails into separate folders.

7. What advice would you give yourself starting out?

Himalee advises that we should not be afraid to take calculated risks. She feels that although we need to do our due diligence first, one's 'gut feeling' is still very important. She further advises that we need to be careful when going into a new area. Australia has so many opportunities, but it is advisable to study the area you are interested in or working in and understand the relevant laws and regulations as there are many little things that can trip you up. She advises that you need to have the knowledge to defend yourself against the 'sharks circling everywhere', and 'know what you are doing so people cannot take advantage of you'.

IV. BUSINESS CASE EXAMPLES

8. Provide a case you managed well and why?

Case 1 – Petrol station/ Mechanical workshop

Himalee's brother, unbeknown to Himalee's family, was working as an apprentice motor mechanic when he was supposed to study engineering at Monash University. He did this because he was a car enthusiast and loved works related to cars. But eventually he revealed his secret to her. He became worried about his job when the owner was going to sell the business while retaining the freehold. Himalee investigated the business opportunity and purchased it in 2004. The business was quite successful and survived challenges from the Covid 19 lockdowns and restrictions. Her brother now has a one-third share, with Himalee and her husband Vijaya owning the other two-thirds. It is an old-style, 'full driveway service' type petrol station with a small retail shop and a mechanical workshop which offers roadworthy certificates, automotive repairs and services, tyres, batteries, gas and ice etc. It was supported by the local community and promoted by Fox FM radio and Channel 9.

In 2008 the owner wished to sell the freehold property. Himalee offered $1.2M which was already a high price, but the owner refused and wanted more. Himalee took advice from one of the authors to appoint a buying agent who was not known to the owner. At the auction, which Himalee did not attend, the buying agent was successful in buying the property substantially less than the original asking price. The owner was furious about this as he expected to obtain a higher premium from Himalee as she had a vested interest in the property. This was Himalee's first business venture and has been a very successful one to date.

Himalee's parents also help in running the business. Their ideas and contributions have been an immense help for the success of the business and freed up Himalee's time for her to take up other challenges.

Figure 7 - Himalee and her brother at the service station

Case 2 – Taprobane Books and gifts

The first ever Buddhist convention in Australia was held in Melbourne in June 2002. Himalee was one of the organising committee members. There was a need to display books on Buddhism written in English at the convention. Himalee formed Taprobane Books and Gifts and imported books from Sri Lanka.

Later she continued the operation of Taprobane Books and Gifts as a home-based business, and it became the sole agent for almost all the major publishers in Sri Lanka.

At the time there was a good demand for Sinhala language books, music CDs, VCDs and DVDs within the Sri Lankan community in Australia. Himalee continued importing those items and sold them from home. Also, she held books exhibitions at Sri Lankan community events to promote the business. Though there is not much demand now, she has still got some customers and import books on demand.

The period between 2010 to 2014 was the peak of when Sri Lankan refugees migrated to Australia. During this period Himalee saw an opportunity to supply books in the Sinhalese and Tamil languages and associated giftware to refugees in government detention centres. This business grew rapidly, and she expanded into other languages including Arabic, Urdu, Hindi, Farsi, Dari, Vietnamese, Mandarin and Burmese etc.

She did not stop there and expanded the services to supply a vast array of items including recreational items such as billiard tables, table tennis tables, carrom boards and commercial grade microwave ovens among other things. This business has levelled off in the past few years.

Authors' note: The success of this business shows the advantage in thinking 'outside the box' and looking at gaps in the market.

Case 3 - Post office

Himalee noticed a post office in close proximity to her petrol station. At the same time her sister was looking for a job. At this stage Himalee was also looking into the viability of investing in an aged care business which her sister could manage. Her sister was initially interested in aged care but later was reluctant because of the strict and detailed regulations involved.

In 2013 Himalee heard that the post office was for sale. She investigated the business and determined that it was a viable business for her family, and the price was less than that of the other similar post offices. An issue was that her sister would need to learn the business and do some unpaid training, but the benefit was that the running of a post office was not as regulated as aged care. After some further investigations she went into the business 50/50 with her sister and brother-in-law. Her sister now draws a reasonable salary, and it has been a good investment. Initially she saw great opportunities for expansion perhaps including a pharmacy. In the end only the giftware side of the shop was expanded. Himalee considered this investment as a calculated risk with capital growth.

Authors' note:

- Employing friends or family can work but there needs to be a very strong understanding of everyone's role and full transparency of how the business works and of course, a high level of trust.
- After buying a petrol station and a post office, Himalee seems to be playing a real life 'Monopoly' game, which means a railway station must be next (☺).

9. Provide a case that did not go well and why?

Case 1

Himalee is a keen accountant and was interested in developing a taxation practice, particularly as a business that she could conduct during her retirement period. To prepare for this she became a signing agent for an accounting practice on a part time basis and to balance her work, she reduced her hours as an employee in the manufacturing company. The owner of the taxation practice unfortunately had a terminal illness, so the power of attorney for the owner had to sell the business. Himalee was quite interested in this opportunity. However, while she was conducting her due diligence, she noticed some serious irregularities in the operations of the practice. She officially reported her findings so that she would not be personally implicated in the wrong-doing, and then backed out of this transaction. Himalee realised that the best thing to do if something is not working properly and is unlikely to be corrected is to withdraw as quickly as possible. Her philosophy is that a small initial loss is better than a later big loss (in terms of dollars, time and especially reputation, both personal and professional).

Case 2

The petrol station business also has a mechanical workshop with the Licensed Vehicle Tester (LVT) licence to conduct roadworthy testing and to issue roadworthy certificates. Himalee's brother is the roadworthy testing mechanic and authorised person to issue roadworthy certificates. Unfortunately, due to a poor driving record he had his driver's licence suspended for 6 months. Himalee later received a letter from the state's roadworthy testing authority suspending the workshop's LVT licence as a result of the suspension of the testing mechanic's driver's licence. This became a big loss to the business as issuing roadworthy certificates had been a major source of the workshop's income. Himalee assumed this was only a temporary suspension and the LVT licence would be reinstated when her brother's driving licence was reinstated. Later she received a letter stating that the workshop's LVT licence had now been cancelled. In the first letter it was stated that she needed to take action to nominate another testing mechanic to keep the LVT license active. Himalee, not being experienced in this area, was confused and did not take any action. As she did not comply with the requirements the LVT licence was cancelled. Himalee unsuccessfully appealed to the authorities, and she was forced to apply for a new LVT licence. It was an expensive and time-consuming process which took 18 months in which full courses and tests and interviews had to be redone. Finally, the licence was regained in 2021.

Authors' note: red tape bureaucracy is the bane of our lives but is often best dealt with using patience and perseverance rather than anger. Said another way, if you do not understand it, get professional help.

10. What conclusions can be drawn by comparing these cases?

These cases highlight the importance of 'local knowledge' and while taking business risks, you must follow through promptly and thoroughly on the high-risk elements of the business venture. This is reflected in the need to examine closely any communication from the regulating bodies for any fine print because dealing with the bureaucracy can be expensive and time consuming if you do not get it right.

The other important lesson is the advantage in working in a business before investing in it. Before buying a business there is a big advantage in working in a similar one first for a while to pick up the nuances. This is especially valid in the more regulated type of businesses, for example petrol retailing (aged care is another one).

11. What cultural issues did you experience? How were they overcome? How is Australia different? Were these cases affected by cultural issues?

Himalee was sponsored by her aunt and uncle and migrated to Australia as a permanent resident. She came to Australia with another aunt and uncle. She had her accounting qualifications but was lacking experience in general business, personal confidence and an understanding of Australian culture. She found that the freedom, openness and humour in Australia took a lot of getting used to. She remembers one time when a staff colleague swore in general business conversation and found this very confronting. She recollected that when someone from management entered her office she used to stand up and call them Mr or Mrs. She quickly realised the informality of Australian culture and adapted to it.

Himalee had an arranged marriage. She says that in retrospect there was more due diligence performed in this, including matching horoscopes and background checks by the respective families and examining of options, than occurred in most marriages, or indeed in most businesses! Himalee says that marriages are much more than just the union of two people involved.

Himalee sees Australia as a land of opportunity, and anyone can achieve success if they are confident and prepared to take some risk. She stated that one big advantage in Australia is the low level of corruption compared to many other countries overseas. She has occasionally felt being looked down, but this has not affected her activities.

Case example

Himalee needed an environmental report for the petrol station as a requirement for bank finance. This is usually obtained every few years at a cost of around $20,000 to $30,000. The relationship manager of the bank (one of the major banks) insisted on an extra environmental report and Himalee had to hurriedly obtain it. Partly due to the rush, the report turned out negative. Under a lot of pressure Himalee was forced to find alternative finance which she eventually did find. Himalee feels there may have been some cultural and definitely sexist undertones in the way she was dealt with.

Authors' note: perhaps lodge complaint with Australian Financial Complaints Authority

On the other hand, Himalee's strong Sri Lankan family culture helped build one of the very few full driveway service petrol stations. Her petrol station has endeared itself to many people including elderly and others who appreciate the service. In some sense their culture has enabled them to be successful and be appreciated by a full range of customers.

V. VOLATILITY (FOR EXAMPLE COVID)

12. How has the virus affected your business?

Himalee has learnt a lot about running a business and understanding how to take calculated risks. All this has helped Himalee to manage the family's various businesses during the 2020-

2021 COVID-19 pandemic. The JobKeeper scheme and the State's business support programs have greatly assisted the petrol station and post office businesses to stay viable. Even though petrol stations and post offices come under essential services, the constant lockdowns during the pandemic made running them during the lengthy lockdowns, loss-making businesses.

13. What lasting impact do you think it will have on your business?

As with many difficult situations the businesses likely to survive are the ones in which the owners search for creative ways to build, adopt and manage their customer base, and especially in difficult times. The COVID-19 pandemic is one such example.

14. What have you learned from it that you will now implement in your business?

She has learned to be more careful with her time. With working routines turned upside down during COVID-19 she has an arrangement with her manufacturing company employer to work at the office only one day per week. This gives her more flexibility and saves on travelling time.

She has also learned to be creative and proactive. With the Post Office business Himalee has seen a significant increase in sending and receiving parcels during the Covid-19 pandemic period which was good for the business. Himalee trialled selling nonstandard items at the Post Office. Interestingly ice-cream has become one of the best sellers.

VI. FAMILY BUSINESS

15. Are you in a family business and from your experience what do you think are the advantages and disadvantages of family working in the business?

Her response as to whether she is in a family business was "Yes – definitely".

She provided the following summary of family business.

Advantages:

- Family members benefit as the wealth is often distributed among the family.
- Less formality in conducting meetings and implementing decisions.
- Family members share the workload and work over and above the normal call of duty under demanding situations.
- Achievements are not measured only by financial means. Working together as a happy family alone is a big achievement.
- Higher resilience under difficult situations – for example, survival under the COVID-19 pandemic situation.
- Easy to make decisions - no red tape.
- Very flexible working conditions.

Disadvantages

- If personalities are not flexible, making important decisions could be hard.
- Serious disagreements could have an impact on family relationships.
- Growth is limited by the motivation of the family members.
- If the business is not expanding and not employing new personnel, the skill set will be limited.
- Some members may not be serious about following guidelines.

- Opportunities and motivation for professional development is limited.
- Going on holidays together as a family will not be easy.

Figure 8 - Himalee receiving her Certificate of Congratulations for Volunteer Services to the Community - April 2021

FUN FACTS ON: BAD PREDICTIONS

On Not Signing The Beatles

Decca Recording Company expressed their opinion on signing the Fab Four in 1962–and it wasn't positive: "We don't like their sound, and guitar music is on the way out." But according to cbsnews.com[1], the Beatles have sold 1.6 billion singles in the U.S. and 177 million albums. So much for guitar music being "on the way out."

On the Popularity of Harry Potter

Publishing executives sounded pretty positive that Harry Potter[2] would be a flop when they wrote this to J.K. Rowling in 1996: "Children just aren't interested in witches and wizards anymore." They probably wish they could use an "obliviate" spell right about now.

On Drafting Michael Jordan

Rod Thorn, the Chicago Bulls[3] general manager, didn't have much hope for Michael Jordan when he said this in 1984: "I wish Jordan were 7-feet. But he isn't. There just wasn't a centre available. What can you do? Jordan isn't going to turn this franchise around…he's a very good offensive player, but not an overpowering defensive player."

On Elvis Presley's Musical Future

Eddie Bond, a radio host, didn't think Elvis would make it as a singer when he said this in 1954: "Stick to your day job. You're never going to make it as a singer." Yet somehow, Elvis still managed to make money after he died, according to forbes.com[4] –

---

[1] *https://www.cbsnews.com/news/the-beatles-by-the-numbers/*

[2] *https://www.readersdigest.ca/culture/must-read-classic-books/*

[3] *https://www.readersdigest.ca/travel/world/top-8-north-american-cities-sports-fans/*

[4] *https://www.forbes.com/sites/kellyphillipserb/2013/08/16/death-and-taxes-elvis-presley-topped-charts-and-tax-brackets/#52e866137c52*

which is strange for someone who apparently wasn't singer potential.

On Ronald Reagan as an Actor

The United Artists executive rejected Reagan as the lead for The Best Man[5], and claimed he didn't have "that presidential look." He ended up being the 40th president of the United States from 1981 to 1989.

On Electing a Female Prime Minister

In 1969, Margaret Thatcher didn't believe that a woman would become prime minister in her lifetime. Ten years later, she became the first female prime minister of Britain from 1979 to 1990, according to biography.com[6].

Source: Readers Digest (2021).

[5] *https://www.readersdigest.ca/culture/highest-grossing-movie-years/*
[6] *https://www.biography.com/people/margaret-thatcher-9504796*

John Engelander

From a computer salesman to the owner of a successful green cleaning business.

INTRODUCTION

Key points from the interview

- To seek clarity, write notes and drill down into your thoughts to try to identify gaps and where possible create a flow diagram to make a road map of the situation
- Difficult times do not build character, they reveal it
- Exercise and meditation can make an enormous difference
- He feels that it is important not to get stifled with over-analysis, but just get started.
- John considers that one must be careful in taking advice only from accountants who are trained to see the risks and pitfalls. John would give young people who are evaluating whether to go into business three things to consider:
    - What are the person's strengths?
    - What do they love doing?

    - Is there a market for it?
- John thinks keeping one's options open is an important lesson, where one needs to be ready for various challenges.

John Engelander

John's journey to find himself led him to realise his passion for the environment, and then combining this with his "street smarts" and entrepreneurial skills, he formed a successful green cleaning company

Further information

- *https://planetearthcleaning.com.au/*

Category

Eco/Green Entrepreneur. *Eco-entrepreneurship, or ecopreneurship, is a business behaviour adopted by people who want to create a "green" business. In other words, it is a way to contribute to sustainable development while making profit (enicbcmed, 2021).*

I. KEY DATES

- John left school to work in his father's importing business packing boxes in the warehouse.
- In 1979 after a few years of being in his father's business, the business collapsed financially. Several jobs later, John started working as an actor, and still gives the occasional performance.
- In 1984 his acting agent introduced him to a commission only sales job with Olivetti, well-known for manufacturing typewriters, and at the time were also the world's second largest manufacturer of personal computers. Within a year John made enough money to buy his first home. Within the first 12 months he decided to employ a person using his commission earnt which enabled John to get on with what

he does best which is to get out and win business whilst his employee was able to follow-up on clients and administration.

- In 1986 at the 18th month point John opened his own IT business, "Automated Office" in Bourke Street in the Melbourne CBD. Within 4 years he became Olivetti's largest re-seller in the country. His government clients always needed 3 quotes and because his service was so good, they told him what the lowest bid was, and he simply came in slightly under that amount. This is how the business grew.
- In 1991 Olivetti lost its market profile and started to sell directly to his clients. Worse still, they then priced their product under John's buy price resulting in John no longer being able to sell at a profit.
- In February 1992 John walked out of his IT business's office for the last time. Everything he built dissolved: no business, property gone and even more devastating his self-esteem. John accepted a job selling computers imported from China.
- Later in 1992: He was approached to help build a cleaning business that had been established for over ten years and started with them. Within 3 months John had grown the business by 50%. One day, one of the cleaners did not show up. John thought that to get a sense of what it felt like as a cleaner he would act as the replacement for the day and rolled up his sleeves. Stuck in a toilet cubical, John proceeded to unscrew the cap of the cleaning chemical and as he did this the fumes were suffocating, and he could barely breathe, and the chemicals affected his skin. It was then that everything would change. He thought "there has to be a better way". He told his business partner that he could replace toxic with non-toxic cleaning products, which would be safer for the staff and environment. Surprisingly, the business partner was not interested. John then decided to start his own company.
- In 1994 he started The Planet Earth Cleaning Company *https://planetearthcleaning.com.au/*. The business became very successful and grew over the years.

- At one stage John was able to sell off a small portion of his business to fund new opportunities. The business kept expanding particularly as the importance of sustainability and green friendly products caught up with John's vision. The business became much more than just a cleaning business to his clients.
- In the intervening years he was involved in some other ventures (see question 10) John likes those interesting start-ups with a point of difference.
- In 2008 he saw that his clients wanted to recycle but were having difficulty doing this, even though the clients had signage on the bins. As a result, John created, "Ecobin", a colour-coded bin system making it simple to separate waste. The tag line was, "Changing your waste habits" (*https://www.ecobin.com.au/*). Over time Eco Bin traded Australia-wide with customers being from a variety of organisations, including Federal, State and Territory and local government departments, schools, universities etc. It was Australia's first colour coded simple and straightforward waste separation system and became very popular in Universities and schools. He even sold a transparent bin system to the MCG (Melbourne Cricket Ground), a very well-known sports arena.
    - Eco Bin, Flip model are assembled by an inclusion workforce. This is another important value of ours: ensuring less advantaged people are given opportunities to work.
    - The cross-selling opportunities of Eco Bin clients to Planet Earth, provides the enormous potential/benefits as the sum of its parts are greater than the whole.

II. GETTING TO KNOW THE PERSON

1. What is success?

John feels that "success is really happiness". John loves what the country Bhutan (a country between Tibet and China) has done in establishing Gross Domestic Happiness, GDH, and not the more usual economic Gross Domestic Product, GDP, as a key measure of country success. John does not really like to use the word "success" as it implies winners and losers. He would much rather use "fulfilment", as fulfilment implies a life balance including:

- Energy level
- Brain stimulation
- Sense of accomplishment

John obtains fulfilment from fun and adventure, making a positive contribution to the world environment. He loves to dance, sing and laugh with his friends and family. He also obtains fulfilment from what he has achieved. John also does not like to use the word "failure" and would prefer to use "a moment when there is a fall" or "a fall" just like when a toddler falls but is determined to use whatever they can to get back up.

2. What is your favourite TV show, movie or book and why?

- Movie – *The Hudsucker Proxy*. This is a comedy starring Paul Newman and Tim Robbins. (It was co-written produced and directed by the creative directors Joel and Ethan Coen)
- Book – *The Fourth Estate* by Jeffrey Archer. The book is based on two real life media barons – Robert Maxwell and Rupert Murdoch, who fought to control the newspaper market.

3. What are your hobbies and/or Interests?

John is a keen student of life philosophy and is keen to create new business ideas. He is keen on taking on new challenges and is currently learning the piano. He is very attracted to Australia's abundant outdoors and is keen on activities such as road cycling, mountain bike riding, dirt bike riding, water skiing and snow skiing.

Authors' note: He also attempted kitesurfing once and John feels that his most epic moment was Heli cycling in New Zealand where he was dropped off at the top of a mountain and cycled to the base.

III. TIPS

4. How did you get through your worst times?

John said that in his hard times he sought clarity, and to achieve this he wrote copious notes, brain dumped, drilled down into his thoughts to try to identify gaps and where possible create a flow diagram so he had a road map of the situation. He said that he often writes down questions that need answering. He would think about where he could gather the necessary resources to ultimately bring together the many parts and create a probable outcome. John also notes that "difficult times do not build character, they reveal it". He feels that exercise and meditation can make an enormous difference and regularly tells himself 3 things:

- He has his *health*
- He remains *calm*
- He seeks *clarity*

5. What keeps you awake at night?

John generally sleeps well. However, what can keep him awake is not having a resolution for a specific issue. On the other hand, staying awake may have something to do with excitement looking forward to a fun activity. Late last year he bought a new road bike, and some days could not wait to ride it, and this kept him awake. He loves the thrill of creating that cycling momentum.

6. What are your typical daily routines?

John does not follow set routines. He has a business compass and knows what is needed. He calls it his "True North". As a result, he prefers to have a more free-flowing lifestyle. He likes not to be under anyone's control. John is usually in bed by midnight and up at 7 am but this varies widely. John does not have an alarm clock and uses his body clock to wake.

7. What advice would you give yourself starting out?

In the beginning, he wishes that he believed in himself more. He says, "do not believe that other people have the same values as you". Unfortunately, one cannot trust everyone, and we are not all the same. John's school days were very mixed, and he transferred from private to public schooling where he saw a big difference. He feels that from his schooling he really only obtained the basic "three R" skills (reading, writing and 'rithmetic), however he realises that he can purchase specialist skills whenever needed. These include legal and business advice, and he once hired a lecturer from Swinburne University to do research and provide information John needed. John also sees that sometimes people can over-think issues. He feels that it is important not to get stifled with over-analysis, but just get started (See Authors' note below). John considers that one must be careful in taking advice only from accountants who are trained to see the risks and pitfalls. John would give young people who are evaluating whether to go into business three things to consider:

1. What are the person's strengths?
2. What do they love doing?
3. Is there a market for it?

John says he does a mini self-evaluation every day working out what he will be doing that day, and this activity fulfills him. He is always looking at something new to keep himself interested.

Authors' note: The authors favourite quote is by Woody Allen who said something to the effect that "80% of success is just turning up".

IV. BUSINESS CASE EXAMPLES

8. Provide a case you managed well and why?

Case 1 – Automated Office

In his 20s John set up his "Automated Office" (see details in Part I, Key Dates above). The early success of this business showed him that he has strength in dealing with people, especially staff and clients. He feels that he can see the different strengths in people and if there is a problem, he has the ability to drill down to determine the root cause. He is not afraid of challenging people to succeed and often encourages staff to be successful. He has carried this strength into his successful cleaning and related businesses. John had the best lessons of his business life in Automated Office and realised how the many parts make a whole business.

Case 2 – Ecobin

The Ecobin project (see details in Part I, Key Dates above) was an amazing almost overnight success. From initial idea to implementation took only 6 weeks. It was a good business idea with the right team of people to see it through to successful implementation. Both Planet Earth and Ecobin tell a story about "why" his clients buy. After all anyone can obtain cleaning services, but his green environmental approach embodies an authentic purpose - a desire to be responsible. After all, as John says, "It's not an investment if we are destroying the planet".

9. Provide a case that did not go well and why?

Case 1 "Automated Office"

This was a successful business for some years but in 1992 it suffered due to changes in the Industry and the inability of the key supplier to move with the market (see details in Part I, Key Dates above).

Cases 2 and 3

When he sees a problem that is not likely to be resolved he has been quick to "cut his losses" to stop it from becoming a major cost. Below are two examples of start-ups he trialled but discontinued. Both ventures stalled partly due to with direction issues between John and the partners in these businesses. The commercialisation stage also presented with issues that were not foreseen. The cases are:

- *Case 2 Aromatherapy. (Through Air-conditioning)*
  The business was providing aromatherapy (which is holistic healing treatment that uses natural plant extracts to promote health and well-being) through air-conditioning systems, for example shopping centres / hotel lobbies where research showed that a pleasant aroma can be a very positive influence on people. John sold out his share due to differences with his partner. The business continued after John left.
- *Case 3 Cleaning software*
  This started as an idea to make inspections and quoting for the cleaning industry more efficient by using a software application. John joined in with a software company to develop this software as a joint venture. This was an outstanding product that unfortunately required constant development costs. When the programmers changed their programming language, the software was no longer compatible, requiring a complete rebuild making the project unviable. John chose not to do this and exited the business. (However, the product was successfully used at Planet Earth Cleaning Company in Beta testing.)

Authors' note: perhaps initial scoping problems?

10. What conclusions can be drawn by comparing these cases?

John notes that perhaps he is best suited to being in control rather than work with one or more partners, at least on a daily working basis. When working with partners he believes that there are two key factors, trust and chemistry. He says that the more control you have over the direction and ownership of the brand the more efficient you can be in investing into its success. John considers that the main lesson to be learnt in the cases in Questions 9 and 10 is that ownership and control of the business/brand is vital.

11. What cultural issues did you experience? How were they overcome? How is Australia different? Were these cases affected by cultural issues?

John considers that there are no cultural issues that affect his business. John advised that as with his answer to Question 8, the above cases have not been affected by any cultural issues. In fact, he welcomes inclusiveness and for this reason believes this one of the reasons he has always had a strong culture within his organisations.

V. VOLATILITY (FOR EXAMPLE COVID)

12. How has the virus affected your business?

Both Eco Bin and Planet Earth struggled as demand for its services have reduced due to the necessity to work from home and the closure of offices and schools.

John is finding it difficult to find enough people to clean for him. However, with perseverance and determination found new ways to add business, forcing him to think outside the box. While clients are re-opening and business is beginning to pick up, he is acutely aware of the need to stay alert and not take business for granted. He stepped up his teams and lifted the spirit of the workers. A proud culture that felt worthy. Planet Earth's, "COVID RESPONSE" cleaning teams have kept their clients safe and, in the process, won new business. Responding quickly to the needs of the market has kept the business strong.

13. What lasting impact do you think it will have on your business?

As a chess player, John thought one could always strategize. However, 2020 showed him business and life can be like poker with the sudden receipt of the COVID-19 "hand". He is proactively adding services to meet the lasting impacts of what many describe as "the new normal". And while business has returned to this new normal, a key issue will be in the medium to longer term whether there will be less occupied office space, resulting in less floor area to clean. For John, this opens new opportunities. He welcomes the challenge.

14. What have you learned from it that you will now implement in your business?

John thinks keeping one's options open is an important lesson. Although we are always facing something unexpected, his is still thinking of his next chess move. Strategy is key.

John believes that you should "never be fixated with uncertainty". It's a stimulus that can bring about new opportunities. Currently Australia has closed borders from overseas workers, and the availability of people to do cleaning is becoming more difficult, and thus it is very difficult to get staff and he is looking at alternatives. Once again, the values and clear purpose of Planet Earth attract talent. That's why he has always believed that a strong sense of purpose is more viable than merely the profit. Purpose first, and profit will come!

VI. FAMILY BUSINESS

15. Are you in a family business and from your experience what do you think are the advantages and disadvantages of family working in the business?

John does not consider his businesses can be categorised as a "family business". John said it may work well, however he once had a family member work for him and found it difficult to manage him due to their relationship. At Automated Office, the business worked well and then he worked with two other people who were brothers, and it created unnecessary chaos in the business. Once they left, the business had once again enjoyed flow and harmony. John felt it was difficult to discipline one of the brothers due to the effect on the other brother. John thinks that working with partners is difficult but can be further complicated if there are also family connections to deal with. He considers that family businesses may work with the right people, with the right attitudes and says that he has seen some of these businesses work well. He further considers that working with family members at a Board level may not be so much of a problem, but day to day dealing can be more complicated.

Figure 9 - The Head OfficeTeam celebrating John's 60th by wearing some of John's favourite slogans - The T-shirts came from Vinnies (Also all cleaners uniforms are "fair trade")

Figure 10 - John Engelander and author Daniel Bendel

FUN FACTS ON: VACUUM CLEANERS AND CLIMATE CHANGE

Vacuum Cleaners

"Nuclear-powered vacuum cleaners will probably be a reality within ten years."

Alex Lewyt, president of Lewyt vacuum company, 1955

- The first known incarnation of an air-dependent cleaner was invented by a carpet sweeper in 1860. Daniel Hess invented a machine in his Iowa workshop that gathered dust using a rotating brush. A set of hand-pumped bellows was used to create the blow dust into a bag, rather than suck it.
- Hubert Cecil Booth is widely regarded as the first engineer to use suction instead of blowing to remove dirt and dust from floors. His "Puffing Billy" created suction by pumping air through cloth.
- During the 1920s, the principle behind Booth's vacuum cleaner was used to develop the first hooded blow dryers in hair salons.
- During the 1920s and 1930s the Hoover Company was the first to make the electric vacuum cleaner appeal to mass markets around the world.

Source: Cleaning Hacks (2021)

Climate Change

Alexander Graham Bell, better known to most people as the inventor of the telephone, made a surprising warning in a 1917 paper. The unchecked burning of fossil fuels would *"have a sort of greenhouse effect,"* he wrote, and it would eventually cause the Earth to become *"a sort of hot-house."* What shall we do, he wondered, in a piece for National Geographic, when all the oil and coal dries up?

His suggestions: Alcohol as an alternative fuel, and devices that would collect solar power from sunlight and use it as an energy source. His ideas didn't get much traction at the time.

Art Phillips (also known as Arturo DiFilippo)

From a musician extraordinaire migrant to the Director, UBSS Centre For Entrepreneurship

INTRODUCTION

Key points from the interview

- When working with partners make sure there is a formal fully documented agreement that specifies the mechanics of what should happen if the partners have a disagreement.
- Art advises the importance of fully scoping out the specific characteristics of the industry you are entering
- A drop in income is not necessarily a bad thing as it can make you investigate new options
- Most problems are temporary and recommends focusing on what you like to do and think, and persevere through the difficult times

- He would advise young people to "enjoy the moment or said another way, to "stop to smell the roses" more than he ever did.

Art Phillips (He is also known by his Italian grandfather's surname DiFilippo, hence Arturo DiFilippo)

A musical performer, musician, composer, musical director, orchestrator and entrepreneur who since the age of thirteen has lived by the three letters "FDP", that is - he seeks to always keep "Focus, Determination and Perseverance" by his side, at his realisation, his motivation and as his reality check.

Further information

- *https://artphillips.com*
- *https://101.audio/bio-art-phillips*
- *https://101.audio/*
- *https://www.ubss.edu.au/art-phillips/*

Category

Part time Entrepreneur/Consultant. Running a business (owner of music production library) whilst working as employee (teaching Entrepreneurship subjects at UBSS).

I. KEY DATES

After an early career in music performing, Art commenced a business of composing and arranging for other artists, film and TV scoring. For over 30 years he has lectured in music composition and performance subjects, as well as business and entrepreneurship subjects at the postgraduate level across various universities and institutes throughout the world. Let us now look at how his career unfolded.

- In the 1960s Art grew up in a musical family, playing guitar and mandolin with his father and grandfather. He was playing guitar at 5, and at the age of 9 he was clear that he wanted to be a guitarist. At that age he wrote a letter to Tony Mottola (1918 – 2004) the well-known American jazz guitarist who released dozens of solo albums, and worked as guitarist for Frank Sinatra, Perry Como, The Tonight Show starring Johnny Carson, and many more. Tony mentored Art by returning every letter Art had written to him, took his telephone calls, and finally in 1982 they met in New York City while Art was performing as guitarist for Barry Manilow, at the Uris Theatre on Broadway. Tony was the second main inspiration for Art and his career, first of which was Art's father, Arthur M Phillips, also a great musician and guitarist.
- In the early 1970s, at the end of high school, he was preparing to study at the Julliard music School of Music in New York City when he was offered an audition for the Lettermen, the 3-piece vocal music group who were famous in the late 60s and 70s. He was chosen and then travelled with the group around the world, including Japan, Philippines, Hong Kong returning to play in his hometown in Erie, Pennsylvania, where he played in front of his family and friends and Lettermen fans. Instead of studying at university he privately studied composition and orchestration.
- In the late 70s and 80s he worked as a guitarist, composer, and orchestrator working and recording for popular artists such as Barry Manilow, Minnie Riperton, Demis Roussos, The Carpenters, Smokey Robinson, Dory Previn, Burl Ives and other well-known artists of that time. He also worked on many television programs and feature films (soundtracks) as recording session guitarist and appeared on-camera as the guitarist on the famous television show *'The Love Boat'*, on some 50 or so episodes during the late 70s.
- In 1980, Art's composition *'Here We Go'*, from recording artist Minnie Riperton reached the top 10 R&B Billboard chart position. The recording was included on her posthumous album Love Lives Forever, Capitol Records.

- Art also co-wrote the original music for the daytime soap opera television series *'Santa Barbara'*, (NBC Television), where he won 2 Emmys for outstanding musical direction and composition in a drama series, 1986 and 1987.
- In 1987 he moved to Australia, as he had many opportunities to broaden his career, such as acting as music composer for the television series *Neighbours* from 1989 to 1991. Much of that music is still re-used today on the series.
- From 1992 to 2000 he served as vice president of the Australian Guild of Screen Composers (AGSC) and was president from 2001 to 2008.
- In 1995 he was awarded the AGSC Award for Best Soundtrack Album for his score to the ABC television series *'The Flying Vet'*, later re-released on all digital stores under the album title *'Native Spirit'*.
- In 2005 he was nominated for an Australian Recording Industry Association Award for Best Original Soundtrack Album for *Outback House* and was nominated in the APRA (Australasian Performing Right Association) / AGSC Screen Music Awards for Best Music in a Television Series or Serial for *Outback House* the series.
- In 2006 his composition *Floating*, sung by American recording artist Megan Rochell, achieved Billboard's Top 40 R & B chart position.
- In 2007/2008 he received nominations for Best Original Music in a Children's Television Series for *Pirate Islands: The Lost Treasure Of Fiji* in 2007 and 2008 at the APRA/AGSC Screen Music Awards.
- In 2010 Art started 101 Music Pty Ltd®, now a successful music production library and label with over 60 record album releases and is represented with distribution across 85 countries under some 25 cross-cultural agreements. When he explains the mechanics of how his music library works (with sub-publishers) he uses "selling shoes" as a metaphor.
- In 2018 he joined the Universal Business School of Sydney (UBSS), where he is a Fellow and sits on the Academic Senate and Course Advisory Committee. In addition to this he is the Chair of Queen Anne School of Management's (QASM) Course Advisory Committee, Deputy Chair of

The Australian Institute of Music's (AIM) Academic Board. He is a recipient of four 'Executive Dean Awards' for 'Outstanding Teaching in the Postgraduate Program' at UBSS. He also lectures in the postgraduate subject *Entrepreneurship Research Report* at UBSS, and in addition has developed, written and delivers, as lecturer, three postgraduate subjects in the 'Music and Media' masters course at Excelsia College, Sydney.

- Since early 2021, Art has been *Director of The Centre For Entrepreneurship* at the Universal Business School Sydney (UBSS).

Figure 11 - Art(right) and his father 1980 playing in Grandpa Antonio DiFilippo's back yard in Erie, Pennsylvania.

In the 1960s Art grew up in a musical family, playing guitar and mandolin with his father and grandfather. He was playing guitar from the age of 5. Art still uses his father's two guitars, both Gibson L-12 f-hole acoustics.

II. GETTING TO KNOW THE PERSON

1. What is success?

Art sees success as being able to follow one's passion which he feels fortunate to have been able to do since the age of 9. He believes his success has come through his continued focus on FDP, his moto, that is "Focus, Determination and Perseverance".

2. What is your favourite TV show, movie or book and why?

- TV: *'Seinfeld'*, and also *'I love Lucy'*, because of the intricate manner in which they deliver their humour and tell their story.
- Movie: All Alfred Hitchcock movies especially *North by North West.* He states that Hitchcock, the movie director, used Bernard Herrmann to write outstanding music scores for his films. Herrmann changed the face of modern musical, textural and emotional drama to feature film.
- Book: *The Violinist of Venice.* This is about Antonio Vivaldi from Venice and his passion for life, music and women, and of course the violin.

3. What are your hobbies and/or Interests?

Art's work is his passion but if he were to choose something outside of his music business, he would choose everything Italian (food, music, language, etc). He energetically took up learning the Italian language in about 2010 and speaks Italian to his relatives whenever he can and travels to Italy regularly. Much of his music has Italian themes.

III. TIPS

4. How did you get through your worst times?

Art admits he takes things personally, "to heart", as he is a passionate person. He realises that most problems are temporary and likes to just focus on what he loves to do and think, and he seeks to persevere through the difficult times. He says that writing and producing music is like meditation. For the past 20 years, his offices and recording studio facility, where he works five days a week and sometimes more, is a commercial property that he purchased. It is located about a 10-minute drive away from his home. It is there that he constructed a soundproof acoustic recording room and a state-of-the-art mix and mastering room. His workplace administration offices are on the second floor of his commercial property overlooking the city.

Figure 12 - Art in his commercial property, inside the recording studio facilities mix and mastering room, which is located just 10 minutes from his home in Sydney, Australia.

5. What keeps you awake at night?

Art feels that he does tend to worry a little and can get frustrated when people do not follow up as he expects, as he is an action man. Sometimes these things can keep him up at night a little, but normally he sleeps very well, regardless of what is happening around him, even if there are issues to resolve – it's like counting sheep he says – the more problems, concerns and worry the more sheep and the faster they go … the quicker he sleeps. His wife says he snores within 3 minutes of hitting the bed. He says that he will leave his observation of her pattern off the record.

6. What are your typical daily routines?

Art has a regular routine. He rises at 6:15am, has a light breakfast and then is in the studio by 7:30am. He is not a regular exerciser, but since the beginning of 2020 he has taken up Pilates and yoga and attends class a few times weekly. He spends time either in the studio or in the office depending on what is happening at the time. He has dinner with his wife around 6:30 in the evening and seeks to be in bed by around 9:30pm.

7. What advice would you give yourself starting out?

Art says that he would not change anything from his early years and said that he would advise young people to "enjoy the moment or said another way, to "stop to smell the roses" more than he ever did. It is also most important for Art to keep passion with everything he does – as passion to him is the forefront of every moment in life. My grandfather used to say to me: "Arturo, whatever you are going to do in life you have to do it 101%, give it your everything and give it your complete passion." Art is a workaholic and does drink a glass of vino and a bit most nights ... after all he says: "Sono Italiano", that is "I am Italian".

IV. BUSINESS CASE EXAMPLES

8. Provide a case you managed well and why?

When Art first started his music library business, 101 Music Pty Ltd, he had to set up a solid sub-publisher network to market his music in each territory and region across the globe. In one territorial instance, Art signed with a large sub-publisher company that was keen to take his product for distribution and licensing, but they did this for their own "multi-brand" strategic purposes, and the deal was not favourable in the end. He advised that organisations do this if they want to create some competition for one or more of their other clients, so that they appear to be competitors. They end up owning multiples and saturate their market – good for them – but not so good for a new boutique music library, as he then become diluted with a massive amount of other music. Competition is good – you just need to gauge how you deal with market saturation.

> **Authors' note:** A "multi-brand strategy" is a business strategy involving a company marketing several similar products as competitors, each with their own individual brand name. This "multi-brand strategy" does have some advantages as a way of securing greater shelf space with little remaining for rival products.

Sometimes sub- publishing companies want certain territories that Art was not happy to give, but he agreed to this on occasion to be able to sign on with a very large multinational organisation. This arrangement can be acceptable, but he could have earned more income in some of the territories that he wanted to give to other smaller sub-publishers. He finally exited this arrangement and commenced individual deals with small sub-publishers in each territory, as he calls the 'indie approach in representation' (that is, the smaller independent companies). Since then, he has built up a solid business comprising well-targeted sub-publishers that have the right "feel" for his music library. They are the ones who work his catalogue and obtain value from his assets. They share a percentage in the asset on a licensing arrangement, therefore it is in their best interests to get use from his music catalogue. He tries to get the best publisher for his needs. He always keeps an eye on the results, which usually takes from 9 months to 18 months to see income results from a music license that happens today.

9. Provide a case that did not go well and why?

At one moment in Art's career, he had a business venture with a partner. While the other partner was keen about the business and its opportunities in the early stages, the partner did not contribute the matching effort that was required to run the company, especially after the first two years of the venture. In addition, the partner was not able to match the investment dollars that were required to propel the company forward, whilst Art continued to fund the company with capital from his personal funds.

After a few years things were falling behind, there was a lack of production output and care from the partner with not much consideration nor respect for Art. The partner was not able to deliver the necessary joint output that is excepted for success and did not understand the inner mechanics of the business even though the partner worked in areas associated with this business type for decades. This was surprising for Art to realise, and extremely disappointing especially as Art was very loyal to their previous working relationship when the partner was a worker in Art's other business.

It was obvious to Art after year four of this venture that this could not continue as it was affecting Art's reputation, as well as his inner passion.

Art had considerable difficulty dealing with this until he made the decision to remove the partner from the company. While this was a relief, it was a stressful process, as they were friends for many years. Art had employed the partner for some 20 years prior as a worker in Arts' main business, yet when bringing that partner into the business itself was not the same as contracting the services as before.

Art no longer believes in 50/50 business arrangements. In marriage and in friendships YES, but in business there needs to be one partner who has a 'veto' advantage. 51/49 % works, as 60/40%, 70/30, etc. Nevertheless, YOU MUST have a partnership agreement, or a business shareholders' agreement in place if you are registering as a company. There needs to be a written document in place to spell out what you will do when something goes wrong, and when you fall out of business love.

Art also concludes that it can be very unfavourable to go into business with friends.

10. What conclusions can be drawn by comparing these cases?

In relation to Question 8 (Provide a case you managed well and why?), Art learnt that there is a place for dealing with large corporates and a place for using smaller "indie" (independent) companies. He believes that over time this may change as there are external threats affecting indies, where these small sub-publishers are beginning to sell out to the large corporates. To protect his interests, he is continually looking for new opportunities and sub-publishers in case this happens to those that he is dealing with. As he owns the copyright as a writer and performer, and also owns the product as a label, his assets guarantee him a certain income stream.

In relation to Question 9 (Provide a case that did not go well and why?), Art has concluded that even 50/50 two-person partnerships are problematic and should have uneven ownership percentages to ensure that only one partner has the right to make final decisions. He said this is to provide some certainty on control and decision making. He felt that there should be a formal fully documented agreement that specifies the mechanics of what should happen if the partners have a disagreement or wish to dissolve the partnership. Art advises the importance of fully scoping out the specific characteristics of the industry you are entering. Take time to read your agreement and do not sign it until you understand its full ramifications.

Figure 13 - "There is only one arrow I like – the one heading northeast!"

11. What cultural issues did you experience? How were they overcome? How is Australia different? Were these cases affected by cultural issues?

When asked about cross-cultural issues he faces, he said that he experiences them every day with his music library business. He said this for two reasons: the first is that he deals with 24 different music sub-publisher agent distributors around the globe, and the second is the language issues. He sighs and says that each territory has different ways of doing things with the biggest cultural issue he faces is the different styles of music preferred around the world. He gives the example that Australian musical tastes are different to Scandinavian, and to Japan or South Korea. He notes that South Korea, which is one of his top territories, likes more upbeat music that can be used for positive advertising for example than dramatic style compositions. In the USA it is more drama style scores that earn the bucks. Art said he cannot always give one territory everything they ask for as it could limit what he can give to other territories. He has a pre-planned album release schedule at least 6 months before the start of each new year, where his company, 101 Music, releases on average 8 new digital albums per year. Each album release contains 12 original main titles (e.g. songs/track/scores), and from each title he also delivers various alternative versions, such as 30s, underscores, stings and various mix-outs. This supplies the client / user, for example the television / film producer and editor, the most diverse possibilities from each track title, increasing the possibility for the highest use from his music. 101 Music is organic and evergreen, meaning that he uses real musicians on all his productions, along with some electronic programming. The benefits of using real musicians on his productions creates a long tail effect, keeping the music product more useful for a longer period as opposed to music being produced with dated electronic type sounds. With this formula in place, his catalogue will not become outdated too soon, as it has much more of a shelf life using real musicians and real instruments.

His company's combined mission and vision statement is:

101 Music Pty Ltd® creates original music uniquely designed for powerful storytelling. Quality, value and artistry are our priorities, delivering 'emotional solutions through music'.

Music is an invisible character, working as a 3rd dimension to define stories. 101 Music Pty Ltd® is a distinctive music catalog that delivers the ambience, the mood, the feeling, the emotion, the tone and the atmosphere you need to propel the stories you want to tell.

'101' focus Keywords: articulate, imaginative, expressive, inspiring, compelling, evocative, intelligent, inventive, unique, original, evergreen, organic.

Art considers that all these business cases were affected by various cross-cultural issues. Even in Australia there can be misunderstandings based on cultural backgrounds. Art advises people to concentrate on their core strengths, and in his case, it is the creator of music and not just as a music publisher. He even has a sub-publisher that represents 101 Music Pty Ltd in Australia and New Zealand, to allow him to concentrate on his own area – the creation and manufacturing and production of music audio product envisioned to be used in film, television, advertising, games and internet audio visuals.

V. VOLATILITY (FOR EXAMPLE COVID)

12. How has the virus affected your business?

Most of Art's income is from copyright content used in film, television and other work rather than performances. Approximately 8% of his music is on radio advertising and the balance in visual content (film, television etc). With the reduction on visual production due to covid restrictions he expected a drop in income. This drop, however, will not be immediate as there is a timing difference between the time a user licenses a song from Art's music catalogue to the time, he receives the income royalties. This is due to the time taken along the various stages from when the music is used to when the publisher receives the royalty, to the time it distributes to 101 Music. In mid-2020, from when COVID-19 really started the affect commerce, he realised that he needed to forecast his income. Projections and assumptions are critical in every business. The first step was to forecast his income for the next 12 months, that is to mid-2021. He forecasted a drop of around 50% to 60%. In mid-2021 he began to see a 20% reduction. Last year Art analysed the business and considered the option of cutting all his production output to zero, as it is expensive to create and manufacture the product, for example the cost of goods sold/direct costs. While that would have saved him some money in the short term, he realised that the effect of this would be that he would not have fresh music releases and resulting in him being pushed down the search engine algorithms losing potential business in the longer term. Instead, he decided to start issuing compilation albums which keep the music releases going and reduces high production costs. This is working and he is happy to see the results.

13. What lasting impact do you think it will have on your business?

He is now planning to continue to issue compilations after every new original album, which he considers will provide him on-going savings. Art thinks that he can continue this strategy for around three more years. He hopes that the pandemic will be finished by then. Foreign publishers seem to like his variety of playlists, for example the compilation album repackaging and releases, thus assisting to extend the life of his music assets.

14. What have you learned from it that you will now implement in your business?

Art says you always need to be evaluating your business and not to be afraid to look into new ideas of trying something different. Also, he says that it is important to plan as soon you are aware of a problem or opportunity. A drop in income is not necessarily a bad thing as it can make you investigate new options. He is always reviewing his sub-publishing relationships, for example his music distributors, and to analysis how they are performing in their own region (territory), and how 101 Music Pty Ltd is performing for them in their territory.

He believes that having the right distributor and sub-publisher is the key to success in each region, and that every territory is not the same as another. His company, 101 Music Pty Ltd, is highly involved with cross-cultural business arrangements and contracts.

VI. FAMILY BUSINESS

15. Are you in a family business and from your experience what do you think are the advantages and disadvantages of family working in the business?

Art advises that his business is not a family business. He uses external contractors in his business. He advises that he is involved in his wife's business which could be seen to be a family business. However, he works in a limited capacity in her business. He has observed other family businesses and sees the inherent difficulties in such an arrangement. He sees separation of family or friend's relationship to the business relationship as vital. In the same way Art built his commercial recording studio facility and offices separate from home to ensure family and work separation. Art says working with family and friends needs a careful base of understanding and sharing of responsibilities.

> The Authors discussed with Art John D. Rockefeller's saying, *"A friendship founded on business is a good deal, and much better than a business founded on friendship"*. That is, if the business relationship is already established then forming a friendship is relatively easy, whereas if you are friends first then you need to establish the business relationship which can be difficult.

Figure 14 - Art Phillips with his Gibson L-12 acoustic guitar built in 1937

Arts' music can be found on all digital stores including Spotify. Some can be found by searching Art Phillips, some Arturo DiFilippo and many others by searching for Art Phillips and the 101 Music Group.

FUN FACTS ON: THE GUITAR

The guitar is the world's second most popular musical instrument, after the piano, and has evolved tremendously over centuries.

The word "guitar" was adopted into English from the Spanish word "guitarra" in the 1600s. Guitars are used in many different genres of music such as: rock, metal, punk, pop, folk, country, traditional, regional, and the blues. Here are some facts about the guitar that you may not know:

- The oldest guitars came from Persia (modern day Iran), about 3,500 years ago, and were called "Tanbur".
- The world's smallest guitar was made at Cornell University in New York. It is 10 micrometres long (1 micrometre is 1-millionth of a metre) with strings 50 nanometres. See photo, below. For your convenience the guitar has been enlarged many, many times!

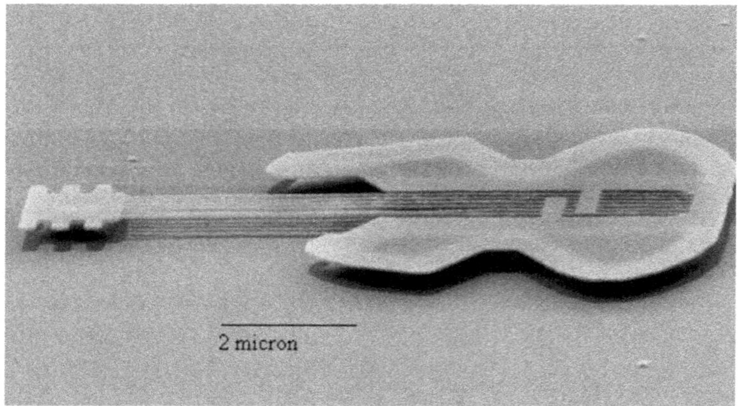

- The design and dimensions of the modern guitar were established by Spanish guitarist Antonio Torres Jurado.
- The Fender factory makes over 90,000 guitar strings a day, that amounts to over 20,000 miles (about 32,000 kilometres) of string per year, enough to circle the Earth.
- Most guitars have 6 strings, but 4 and 12 string guitars are fairly common, and 7, 8, and 10 string guitars are rare but exist. Guitar strings today are made from either steel or nylon. Formerly, they were made from animal intestines.

- The first electrically amplified guitar was invented by musician George Beauchamp and electric engineer Adolph Rickenbacker in 1931. An electric guitar utilises electromagnetic radiation to convert vibrations of its metal strings into electric signals.
- Jimi Hendrix, widely considered the most famous and influential guitarist of all-time, played a right-handed guitar upside down and strung in reverse, because he was left-handed. He even played guitar with his teeth and behind his back! See the 1970 Woodstock film and you will see how good he was.

Source: Sheet Music Plus (2021)

Alice Needham and Philip Chaplin

From selling wraps to manufacturing dog treats for pet food shops

INTRODUCTION

Key points from the interview

- Celebrate the little wins. For example, a new customer, a new successful product, something to keep you going is a great feeling of success. These things keep the business interesting.
- Their philosophy is to make their decisions and then make the most of the outcomes.
- They also have learnt to cut losses early if it appears things are not working out.
- They are very aware of the importance of listening to their customers more and talking less.
- They recommend you explore the industry thoroughly first before going into it to find out all the nuances involved. Try gaining real hands-on experience first

Alice Needham and Philip Chaplin

Entrepreneurial spirit is in their blood. They love the thrill of building a business.

Both Alice and Philip have come from serial business families. They have grown up with this and love the feeling of independence to do their own thing, recognising it still takes a lot of work.

Further information

- *https://wagalot.com.au/*

Category

Serial/Mature Entrepreneur. Someone that has had a background in a variety of businesses and developed a vast amount of experience. Eventually they may become a more mature entrepreneur, See link; *https://www.abc.net.au/news/2021-05-19/older-people-senior-entrepreneurs-successful/100147350* (Why mature-aged entrepreneurs are more successful than their younger counterparts);

I. KEY DATES

- In 1989 Phillip's family sold its hotel. He worked in the hotel and then worked for a catering company.
- In 1989 at the 1989 Melbourne Cup, he met Alice, who was also working there. Alice had worked for Snap printing (her family's business) prior to this for several years. Her parents had several businesses over the years.
- In 1991 Alice and Philip started a new business together in outdoor gardening maintenance called "Don River".
- In 1992 they wound down "Don River" and started a new business "Rain and Shine" irrigation and gardening lighting.
- In 2000 they sold Rain and Shine business, and started a new business called "Wrap Attack" which was a take-away food business in Geelong (in Victoria) with a difference, the difference being that- specialising in creative food wraps.

- In 2005 they moved the "Wrap Attack" business to Bay Street Brighton (in Melbourne) but found there was too much competition for food. While they had an innovative idea, it was difficult to market this amongst the variety of "take-aways."

Authors' note: perhaps they needed a Ray Croc (McDonald's entrepreneur

- In 2010 they converted the Wrap Attack business to a pet shop specialising in bakery items made on the premises. The business was called "Diamond Dog Food and Bakery."
- In 2011 Alice and Phillip started marketing Diamond Dog products on television, and through the newspaper & radio. An unexpected result of this marketing was the request to write a dog cookbook, which ended up being called "Doggylicious".
- This was the television show that prompted the book. *https://www.youtube.com/watch?v=fc5qUeCVRwQ*
- For further information see:
    - *https://www.youtube.com/watch?v=9r9WCMqdOK8&t=322s*
    - *https://www.youtube.com/watch?v=io4NrGHnDKA*
- In 2013 they commenced production on a wholesale basis to retailers. Success followed quickly with sales of specialty Halloween & Christmas dog treats to Petbarn (Australia's biggest pet food retailer).
- In 2015 they relocated to a small factory / warehouse in Seaford (a Melbourne southern bayside suburb) to focus full time and completely on wholesale.
- In 2016 they changed the name of their business to Wagalot.
- In 2017 they relocated to larger premises in Carrum Downs, a suburb near to their Seafood factory.
- In 2020 Alice and Philip wanted to set up a charity to promote the welfare of animals. They established the Wagalot Animal Welfare Fund which is incorporated under the Lord Mayor's Charitable Trust structure and the donations are tax deductible. On many of their products

they give a set amount of the sale proceeds to the charity. They, the staff, friends and family all donate as well. *https://wagalot.com.au/wagalot-animal-welfare/*

Today the Wagalot business, *https://wagalot.com.au/* has become a very well-established pet treat manufacturing company that specialises in unique fun food for dogs. They are now one of the biggest suppliers in their niche business segment to pet food retailers around Australia and New Zealand and are occasional suppliers to major supermarkets. Their business is a good example of a small business that has employed many people over the years (including Alice and Philip, and the loyal taster, see photograph, below), and it has been a model contributor to the Australian economy. They pride themselves on their business ethics and bringing their staff along as a team effort.

Figure 15 – Alice, Philip and the senior taste tester Cliffy (a loyal employee)

II. GETTING TO KNOW THE PERSON

1. What is success?

- *Philip*: The first couple of years in a small business success can be seen as survival, which can be defined as "the ability to spend say $500 on the business without worrying", and this is a great feeling. He also sees success as being able to earn a living and see growth in the business.

- *Alice*: She loves the little wins. For example, a new customer, a new successful product, something to keep them going is her feeling of success. These things keep the business interesting.

Authors' note: the occasional good golf shot keeps him going too!

2. What is your favourite TV show, movie or book and why?

- TV series: "*Line of Duty*" and similar Police crime shows – they both like this and watch together.
- Movies – Different tastes here:
    - *Alice*: more arthouse movies also Coen brothers' movies (quirky and entertaining), movies by Director Wes Anderson.
    - *Philip*: more old movies, including *The Godfather*, *Casablanca.*
    - Both: Grand Budapest Hotel.

3. What are your hobbies and/or Interests?

They said that the business is their hobby, perhaps because they are always together with little other distractions. They see Wagalot as their last business before retirement so are focusing hard on it. They see it as a way of life. Their hours are essentially extended office hours Monday to Friday, and they try not to work too much on weekends. They might talk business for an hour at night. They are up at 5 to 6 am, checking emails then breakfast. Their work hours are:

- *Alice* 7 am to 4 pm
- *Philip* 8 am to 5.30 pm

They travel separately to work because they have different tastes in music. Alice likes triple J, Philip like Classic FM.

Authors' note: maybe a reason to get some alone time ☺

III. TIPS

4. How did you get through your worst times?

They have learnt to "rock and roll with the punches" over the years. Their philosophy is to make their decisions and then make the most of the outcomes. They also have learnt to cut losses early if it appears things are not working out. They are very aware of the importance of listening to their customers more and talking less.

Authors' note: Amen to that ☺

5. What keeps you awake at night?

It has taken time, but they now do not worry about the business at night. However, they may be on edge if there is a big meeting scheduled the next day, for example with a major category buyer, but they do not feel under any real pressure.

6. What are your typical daily routines?

They are up at 5 to 6 am, checking emails then breakfast. Philip takes Cliffy, the golden retriever, for a walk every morning for 40 minutes, and Alice often takes the dog in the afternoon as well. Alice likes to get to work 40 minutes before staff so she can set up everyone's work routines for the day before she gets interrupted. As stated in Question 3, they have a standard daily routine.

Authors' note: Lucky Cliffy!

7. What advice would you give yourself starting out?

Do not go into business unless you are serious about it and can provide the resources required. They recommend you explore the industry thoroughly first before going into it to find out all the nuances involved. Try gaining real hands-on experience first. They said that you need to ensure you have the necessary skills, and particularly good communication and people skills. Imitating others is not necessarily the way to go, and a little imagination can be very beneficial to find your competitive advantage.

IV. BUSINESS CASE EXAMPLES

8. Provide a case you managed well and why?

The case is both an example of a case that went well and one that did not go so well. Alice and Philip had worked to get into a major supermarket. After many meetings and product presentations they finally received an order for a special Christmas product. They were aware of the many horror stories of suppliers being taken advantage of by the big majors, particularly on the "sale or return" of new product placement. They were careful to cover key eventualities, that is supply terms were carefully reviewed, product production and quality were carefully monitored. They had a good contact with the supermarket, and they communicated clearly and constantly throughout the process. The product was then produced over many months and delivered on time and payment was made. This was a successful product sale for two reasons: (1) attention to detail on all the processes; and (2) communication throughout with all key people along the way.

9. Provide a case that did not go well and why?

The supply agreement with the supermarket just discussed above stated that any product not sold by strict cut off dates were to be marked down and the markdown amount was to be shared between Wagalot and the supermarket depending on when marked down according to a set formula. This is a standard supply clause and Alice and Phillip were confident that this should not be a major issue as they were very confident of their product and processes. They had sold similar product before through other avenues and knew at the right price point it would sell well.

What they had not counted on was the complex and bureaucratic internal communications within the supermarket. As this product was not a normal standard product the warehousing and merchandising departments did not get the right internal communications from the buying department on when it needed to be delivered and how it was to be merchandised. As a result, the product was held up in the warehouse and did not go to the actual supermarket until weeks after they were supposed to, leaving an impossibly short time for the product to sell in store. In addition, the "visual merchandising" was left to each store to manage and display the product. In many cases the product was not displayed at all or placed in bad or inappropriate positions. They continually appealed to their supermarket contact who was unable to assist as it was not in their specific "remit" (or authority level). Many of the supermarket computer inventory screens showed the product was in store but when Alice and Philip physically checked the actual store the product was not on display. As a result, there was excess stock at the strict Christmas cut-off date and the supermarket immediately applied the high mark downs resulting in much of the profit needing to be paid back.

Authors' note: In retrospect they should have had ensured this aspect was covered better either by a better markdown clause or a specific clause that any delays of distribution within the supermarket would be allowed for in the calculation. However, it is hard to foresee all these risks in advance, but they are aware of this risk now, and can seek to mitigate the risk in future contract negotiations.

10. What conclusions can be drawn by comparing these cases?

Alice and Phillip firmly believe that from their experience there is a different ethos and way of thinking in small business versus large corporates. They believe that this requires an understanding of the way large corporate business think.

They consider that large corporates tend to use their own jargon, and this can be a barrier to small businesses wishing to engage with them. In a small business often, multiple people understand most of the operations whereas in large corporates work duties are specialised which is understandable give the scale of a large business. However, this means that a small businessperson may need to go to several different people to get an issue resolved. Unfortunately, when seeking a resolution, one often ends up dealing with staff who cannot give an answer even assuming they have the time to assist. In this case the large corporate buyer has the power to order a new product line but then has no further authority or responsibility to help with the success of the product. The corporate buyer would simply discontinue the line if sales were not sufficient. While Alice and Philip do not regret this unfortunate contract with the supermarket, they advise that it is not always a good idea to say "yes" to an offer to sell to a large buyer, such as a supermarket, and sometimes it is best to say "no" if the risks or downsides are too great.

11. What cultural issues did you experience? How were they overcome? How is Australia different? Were these cases affected by cultural issues?

They have not experienced any cross-cultural problems on a non-business level. They have had staff with a range of backgrounds, for example the Philippines, Cambodia etc. with no issues. Dealing with suppliers from India and China and selling into Hong Kong and Singapore requires an understanding regarding the differences in the interpretation of the language and cultural aspects. This requires some experience. They have, however, experienced a significant cultural difference between small business and large corporate business, and this is further discussed in Question 10.

V. VOLATILITY (FOR EXAMPLE COVID)

12. How has the virus affected your business?

The Covid pandemic, particularly the 2020 and 2021 lockdowns in Melbourne, has had many varied effects on every aspect of their business. While they were classified as an "essential provider" (welfare of animals) meaning that they could continue to work during the long Victorian COVID lockdowns, their business was disrupted due to the inability to obtain supplies and the inability to fully work with staff caused by the staff distancing restrictions. This presented many challenges for day-to-day operations when trying to operate their business.

From a business perspective there was an initial sales downturn as stores were running down stocks. However, soon after the initial downturn sales increased as businesses sought to increase their inventory. Therefore overall, there was only a small downturn effect on their business. As Wagalot is focused on the more discretionary end of dog treats, it is unfortunate that during periods of uncertainty consumers purchased less of these products. On the other hand, however, there was a big increase in animal ownership and consumers were not spending on other discretionary purchasing, for example travel.

13. What lasting impact do you think it will have on your business?

As their Industry was not badly affected, they consider that there will be no lasting impact on the business.

14. What have you learned from it that you will now implement in your business?

They have learnt about risk management for a pandemic, so they understand how to follow the rules on COVID-19 distancing, signage, cleaning and associated protection measures. They have certainly learnt to be more flexible on government regulations and how quickly they can change.

VI. FAMILY BUSINESS

15. Are you in a family business and from your experience what do you think are the advantages and disadvantages of family working in the business?

Yes, it is. This is because the owners, Alice and Phillip are not only life partners, but also owners and work together.

Alice and Philip have had limited experience in working with relatives. Their nephew worked well with them, but they needed to set ground rules and separate work from family. It could have been a problem had they not done this. They said that they are wary of bringing in other family members to the business and would prefer not to take this risk.

Figure 16 - Presenting Wagalot novel dog treats on television. Alice is on the left, jokingly offering a dog biscuit to the television presenter.

Authors' note: Danny invited Cyril over to his house and offered him a hot drink and a biscuit. Cyril did not know it was a dog biscuit and when asked Cyril remarked that the biscuit tasted good, except that it was a bit hard on the teeth! What does Cyril eat at home?

FUN FACTS ON: PETS AND ANIMALS

- *"Never stand between a dog and the fire hydrant."*, **John Peer**
- *"The average dog is nicer than the average person."*, **Andy Rooney**
- *"The better I get to know men, the more I find myself loving dogs."*, **Charles De Gaulle**
- *"Properly trained, a man can be dog's best friend."*, **Corey Ford**
- *"The great pleasure of a dog is that you may make a fool of yourself with him, and not only will he not scold you, but he will make a fool of himself too."*, **Samuel Butler**. (See image below for how this works!)

Figure 17 - A dog and his man!

Greg Whateley

From muso to maestro

INTRODUCTION

Key points from the interview

- The difference between an entrepreneur and an intrapreneur
- The importance of "skin in the game" (and the importance of being there and be involved)

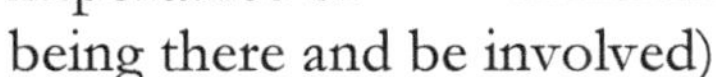

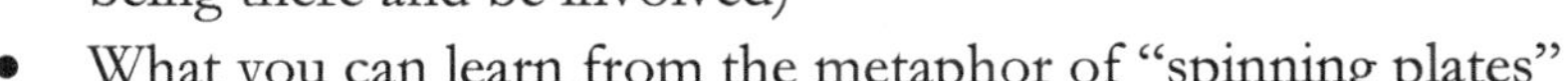

- What you can learn from the metaphor of "spinning plates"
- Beware of different cultural issues when dealing with legal matters
- Have sufficient working capital to allow for volatility in the business

Greg Whateley

He is always looking for new opportunities for development, which he sees as the calling of an intrapreneur (or also known as an "in-house entrepreneur"). He is Mr Spinning Plates", as he uses his "spinning plates" analogy to run successful businesses. See below for further explanation of his "spinning plates" analogy.

Further information

- *https://www.ubss.edu.au/our-people/emeritus-professor-greg-whateley/*

Category

Intrapreneur. *An "intrapreneur" is an entrepreneur who starts ventures from within larger companies. They run the business as if it is their own, but it is not theirs. They:*

- *are involved with entrepreneurial activities within a company that receive organisational sanction and resource commitments for the purpose of innovative results.*
- *Infuse entrepreneurial thinking into large bureaucratic structures, including corporations and governments.*
- *Are known as 'corporate entrepreneurs' in the US.*

I. KEY DATES

- 1954: Born in in Melbourne
- 1975: Diploma of Teaching (focusing on Music and Psychology)
- 1985: Bachelor of Education (focusing on Music)
- 1989: Master of Education (focusing on Assessment and Evaluation)
- 1990: Graduate Diploma in Educational Administration (focusing on Organisational Behaviour)
- 1991: Married to Gabrielle (has two daughters)
- 1997-1999: Academic Manager – Professional Initiatives Unit – *Griffith University, Queensland*
- 2000: To remain with secure employment he declines an offer from Pearson PLC, the listed global English publisher to the Australian and Oceanic manager of their Financial Times Knowledge (FTK) division.

- 2003: Doctor of Professional Studies (focusing on Virtual Pedagogy)
- 2000 - 2003: Head – School of Arts, *Central Queensland University*; Associate Professor and Director – *Central Queensland Conservatorium of Music*; Manager - Business Initiatives, *Faculty of Education and Creative Arts* – Central Queensland University.
- 2004 - mid 2005 Professor and General Manager – *The Australian Institute of Music*, Sydney
- 2005 - 2007: Director, Education and Quality– *National Centre for Language Training – University of New South Wales (Sydney)*; Chair – *UNSW Global eLearning Steering Group*; Chair – *UNSW Global Strategic Improvement Project*; Chair – *Wesley Institute Academic Board* (2007 – 2008)
- 2008 -2010: Principal and Professor – *Australian International Conservatorium of Music* (incorporating *Australian International Performing Arts High School*); Consultant – Creative Industries - *University of Western Sydney College*; Consultant – Graduate Studies - *The Australian Institute of Music*; Consultant – Master of Music – *Wesley Institute*
- 2011-2014: Deputy Dean – *UWS College, University of Western Sydney*; Chair – Academic Board – *Australian Institute of Music*
- 2014-early 2016: Dean and Professor – *The College, Western Sydney University*; Chair – *UBSS Academic Board*; Chair – Academic Board - *Australian Institute of Music*; Chair – *Musicum20 International Music Symposium*
- 2016-2020: - Executive Dean – *Universal Business School Sydney*
- 2020: Greg is currently the Deputy Vice Chancellor at *Group Colleges Australia*. In July 2019 he was appointed Emeritus Professor.

II. GETTING TO KNOW THE PERSON

1. What is success?

Greg sees success as establishing new initiatives that reach fruition and achieve two things: (1) demonstrate a good return on investment; and (2) provide a quality outcome, which is evidenced by objective statistical analysis, student feedback and

Commonwealth government QILT (Quality Indicators for Learning and Teaching) surveys.

Due to Greg's direct involvement UBSS's QILT scores are now well above the National average. Greg is an advocate of Lord Kelvin, the Irish Engineer, who wrote "What you can't measure you can't manage". Peter Drucker, the well-known American management theorist, was in the latter part of the twentieth century a great advocate of this same philosophy.

2. What is your favourite TV show, movie or book and why?

- TV Program: Greg's favourite TV show is *NCIS* – tracking down the bad guys using a mix of 'gut', teamwork and technology.
- Movie: Greg loves the *Da Vinci Code* movie and likes to compare the movie to the book. He likes the intrigue of the storyline. He has visited many of the spots in the movie. He also likes the similar *Angels and Demons* book which is a sequel to the Da Vinci Code film.

3. What are your hobbies and/or Interests?

Greg has little in the way of hobbies other than collecting wine for his cellar. He has about 800 bottles. Work has always served as both entertainment and focus for him. Although he is a trained and skilled musician, and worked as a professional musician, he does not see music as a hobby but rather another enjoyable aspect of business. He tells the story of when running the Central Queensland Conservatorium, the Conservatorium had a $500,000 piano in its own room. He used to get into work early to play it. He saw this as a perk of the job.

III. TIPS

4. How did you get through your worst times?

Greg considers that when the going gets tough one needs to focus, stay calm and put in the extra hours needed. One of his students was having difficulty in completing their work and Greg tells of how he told this student Rob, now a successful university academic, "to sleep less and work more". Greg offered the following tip: "Work hard and be good to your mother". That is, think of your parents and thank them for all the sacrifices they have made for you, and your siblings.

Authors' note: All jokes aside we all need a reason to get out of bed or otherwise we can have too much time for worry.

5. What keeps you awake at night?

He responded: "Nothing really".

Figure 18 - Greg relaxing in Paris in pre-COVID-19 days

6. What are your typical daily routines?

Greg considers that he has a standard routine. After a day's work there is dinner, he watches NCIS with family members and then in bed by 10 pm. He is up at 5 am the next morning and spends the first 4-5 hours of the day working through emails and outstanding tasks and prefers to complete outstanding issues early before meetings. He believes in standard routines as a way of helping him run the organisations that he controls. He uses the "spinning plates" metaphor, which is his way of saying that a leader must do enough to keep everything running smoothly and do not touch the things that are spinning (working) well.

There are exceptions to the above standard daily routine. An example is when he overviews a number of international programs, where he needs to be available during a far wider range of hours to fit in with overseas time scheduling.

Figure 19 - The "spinning plates"

The "spinning plates" image was burnt into Greg's consciousness during a visit to Shanghai where a street performer had some 20 or so spinning plates operating outside a shopping mall entrance. Transfixed, he realised it was a metaphor, in fact, for running a successful business. It was a matter of maintaining a complex set of elements all spinning without falling. On closer examination the performer's management of the plates was the essence of quality management – touch only the sticks (poles) of the plates that looked as though they were waning – leave the others alone. Good management then is knowing which plates (poles) to gently massage – and which to leave alone.

7. What advice would you give yourself starting out?

Focus from the start. Work out what is important and what is not, and what you can achieve and what you cannot. He reminds us of the saying, "Know what you can control and what you cannot and have the wisdom to know the difference".

Figure 20 - Greg pondering the next project

He said that when he was young, he perhaps tried to do too much. For example, he worked in several business improvement roles and then moved on once he had implemented the improvements. Along the way he realised that a good manager should not mess with things that work, and this realisation was the genesis of his "spinning plates" philosophy.

IV. BUSINESS CASE EXAMPLES

8. Provide a case you managed well and why?

In 2015 Greg joined Universal Business School of Sydney (UBSS, see *www.UBSS.edu.au*) which is a Division of Group Colleges of Australia (GCA) as Chair of the Academic Senate and in 2016 transferred full-time as Executive Dean. During that time, he grew the business from 400 students to 1650 students, with 60% of them being postgraduate. Greg feels that this is a good example of strong leadership, industry knowledge and team effort to think creatively to obtain growth and quality outcomes. Greg had previously accomplished a similar successful result with The College at the University of Western Sydney (UWS).

Authors' note: When we asked how UWS fared since he left, Greg noted that he sees no benefit in looking back. He prefers to concentrate on the present and future.

9. Provide a case that did not go well and why?

Case study 1 – as an intrapreneur: "the Japanese program"

Greg ran a graduate program in Film and Television Music in Tokyo Japan on behalf of a local Japanese university for two years. He never visited the site. He essentially sub-contracted the program. Greg feels that the program may have failed because of the lack of his day-to-day attention and personal involvement. Normally Greg would invest his time and energy in running programs to make sure they grow, including communicating with the people directly and would meet with them regularly. However, due to Greg's heavy workload in Australia, and the time drain of needing to spend a day travelling each way to Tokyo he deferred the travel. The program eventually petered out. Compounding the matter was the cultural issue in the way that contractual matters were dealt with. Greg's employer's solicitors provided a 30-page detailed contract with the usual "remedies for breach" and "damages" which are normal in the English-based commercial contract world, such as Australia, but were frightening to a Japanese college head who obviously had not had much contact with Western commerce. It is interesting to note that Greg was looking at a similar project in Singapore but this time he advised the Singapore college Principal to use the Principal's own lawyers to write the contract. Greg learnt from his experience and the Singapore project was a great success. It expanded to the Singapore military but did not proceed due to the Asian Financial Crisis in the late 1990s.

Case study 2 – as an entrepreneur: "Hector the Cat"

In Greg's early career he was offered the job of writing the "Hector the Cat" song for a road safety campaign. See image and link below. He received a very large fee for this song. After this success Greg was very confident that he had a career in writing music and promptly resigned from his university position. After four months obtaining no further work, he realised how difficult it was to make a living in the music industry, and went to see his old boss to ask if he could rejoin the university. It is interesting to note that his former employer laughed when Greg returned stating that he knew that Greg would be back, and kept his resignation in the desk drawer and then handed it back to Greg who tore it up. The advertisement was extremely successful and ran all over the world. Greg noted that had he been on a royalty payment basis he would have earned millions!

Figure 21 - Hector the Cat advertisement: Link: https://www.youtube.com/watch?v=2JXCezYlPNE

From this experience Greg learned that stable employment has its advantages. In the 1990s Cyril Jankoff was completing his MBA and became friendly with the management of the UK listed global publishing company Pearson PLC. Pearson advised Cyril that it was looking for senior management staff to open their Asia Pacific regional office in Melbourne in early 2000. Cyril agreed to attend a meeting with the UK staff when they came to Melbourne to recruit. Cyril and Greg both attended the meeting and Greg was offered the position of Australia and Oceania regional manager for

Pearson's Financial Times Knowledge (FTK) division relating to the sale of Person's accumulated knowledge to universities. Greg considered the offer but declined it stating that he did not want to give up a secure university position for such a new position with no guarantees of future employment. FTK then offered the position to Cyril. Greg was very sensible because within two years the office closed due to unviability of the product in the Australia and Oceania oceanic region. Cyril returned to his business education and consulting practice. Except for his short time as a self-employed songwriter, Greg has never deviated from working entrepreneurially for others.

10. What conclusions can be drawn by comparing these cases?

Greg considers that there are two conclusions:

- The first is that success is about being there, physically and mentally and having what is colloquially known as "Skin in the game".

> Skin in the game: The origin of the phrase comes from southern derby races in the USA. The owners of a horse have "skin" in "the game". As the owner, they have the most riding on the outcome of the derby event.
>
> Steve Jobs humorously explains his version of "skin in the game" *https://www.youtube.com/watch?v=4n6LrehCPOQ*

- The second conclusion is the importance of being aware of the different cultural attitudes. In the Japanese case it was the different attitude to legal contract formats.
- With regard to creative endeavours (that is Hector) – always get yourself a good lawyer and a solid contract.
- Manage your risks proactively.

11. What cultural issues did you experience? How were they overcome? How is Australia different? Were these cases affected by cultural issues?

Greg has taught and/or researched in four Australian States and five countries. He has lead programs in four countries. He has experienced a range of differences but has always been able to work closely with partners and overcome any obstacles. He is closely aware of cultural issues because in addition to the above when he worked at the National Centre for Language Training at the University of New South Wales, they received a $7- 8 Million Federal grant to assist exporters understand foreign culture.

Greg notes that humour and behaviour often do not translate across cultures well, and each culture has its own peculiarities and subtleties. He remembered a joke about a grasshopper that always gets many laughs in Australia, and indeed he told the joke when interviewed in an ABC radio interview, where the laughter interrupted the interview. However, when he told it in Japan there was not a single laugh. The joke was an example of the fact that many things do not translate. The joke was: *'A grasshopper goes into a bar in Tokyo – the bartender says we have a drink named after you – the grasshopper replies – what Shintaro?'*

Greg also advises that often the way that negotiations are conducted, and how you behave in them, is culturally specific, and thus it is important to understand this. For example, he was involved in a Middle Eastern deal where an offer was made, and he later realised some of the aspects of the offer were not negotiable due to their culturally specific background. It is also a culture where 'yes' does not necessarily mean yes.

Apart from the contractual issues mentioned, Greg found no significant issues in dealing with different cultures.

V. VOLATILITY (FOR EXAMPLE COVID)

12. How has the virus affected your business?

UBSS has suffered in terms of international student numbers – but otherwise has fared remarkably well. Not a single member of staff has directly or indirectly been retrenched or made redundant as a result of COVID-19, which is a strong result compared to many other educational institutions.

UBSS invested heavily into technology with moving cameras and associated support technology. This made the on-line experience interesting and life like – no boring lecturers standing in one spot and lecturing the whole time. This classroom style experience of the on-line learning led to high quality education and high student satisfaction survey results. The advantage UBSS has is in its successful hybrid model of in-house and online learning. The COVID-19 virus was a disaster, but it did not have to mean failure.

13. What lasting impact do you think it will have on your business?

The shift to online learning (accompanied by blended learning) will stay with them for some time. In many ways the shift is a game-changer. This is discussed in a number of articles Greg has published in *Campus Review* throughout 2020 and 2021.

There may well be other long-term effects such as being acclimatised to replacing face-to-face meetings with on-line meetings savings substantial costs and travel times. It will present challenges for teaching modes and the need to come up with entertaining and engaging options.

14. What have you learned from it that you will now implement in your business?

Greg thinks the main learning is that you need to move quickly when circumstances change. Many businesses run a risk register and even have a comprehensive crisis response strategy but would still not have been ready for the COVID-19 crisis which was like a sledgehammer. Will businesses relax back within few years? Perhaps. Greg says it is imperative to have sufficient working capital to manage the ups and downs of businesses. This was vital with the COVID-19 crisis. Many businesses will not have had the financial strength to be able to recover after the government support finished.

VI. FAMILY BUSINESS

15. Are you in a family business and from your experience what do you think are the advantages and disadvantages of family working in the business?

The answer to the first part of the question is that Group Colleges of Australia (GCA), is owned by the Manly family and it employs family members, but Greg is not a part of the family, but he has the unofficial title of being the in-house entrepreneur for the Manly family business. He gets on well with the Manly family members who treat him as if he is part of their family.

The answer to the second part of the question is that GCA is a family business which has done well. Greg thinks families can operate a business, or businesses, and succeed. He also thinks a smart family business includes quality support people who know what they are doing. This "family" culture can extend to a kind of "extended family" of long-standing friends and business associates. Many successful businesses seem to have this "family feeling" embedded in the business.

Greg has had an extraordinarily successful career as an "in-house entrepreneur" (*intrapreneur*). He has always treated the businesses and their resources as if they were his own. This effectively gives him the important feeling of having "skin in the game".

Figure 23 - Greg and the Prime Minister Scott Morrison

Figure 22 - Greg and the real boss - Gabrielle

FUN FACTS ON: WINES

Figure 24 - Greg advises against drinking on the job

- Grapes are the most planted fruit all over the world.
- A ton of grapes can be produced into 720 bottles of wine.
- To quench their thirst, people drank wine instead of water centuries ago. During that time, water wasn't clean all the time, and natural fermentation, when the wine is made, could kill germs caused by typhi (salmonella) and cholera.
- It is hard to believe, but some people have a "fear of wine," and it's called oenophobia.
- During the early Roman times, it was forbidden for women to drink wine. Wives who were caught by their husbands drinking wine could be killed if caught in the act.
- Women are more susceptible to the effects of wine than men. It's partly due to biology, as women have fewer enzymes in the stomach lining required to break down alcohol.
- In ancient Greece, the host of dinner would take the first sip of wine to assure that the wine served to guests wasn't poisoned. The act of courtesy was where the phrase "drinking to one's health" originated.
- There are 10,000 varieties of wine grapes existing worldwide.
- "Aroma" is the term for the fragrance of young wine, while "Mellow" is for old wine.
- Wine tasters "swirl" the wine in their glass to release its aromas. They don't also fill the glass more than a third full to leave a space where these aromas can collect.

- A glass of good wine has a lengthy, more lingering aftertaste.
- At a wine-tasting event, it is okay to spit the wine out. When attending such events, it is acceptable to take a sip of wine and hold it in your mouth for a few seconds and then decide to swallow or spit it out. It also allows guests to taste multitudes of wine without getting drunk.
- The largest bottle of wine is the "Nebuchadnezzar." It equates to 20 regular-sized bottles or around 15 litres.
- The biggest producers of wine are Italy, France, Spain, USA, Australia, Argentina and China
- China is the leading market for red wine. It's not only because of the flavour, but the red colour of the wine is considered lucky in Chinese culture and is favoured by the government.

Robert Roshan

From migrant to Founder of Byte IT consultancy

INTRODUCTION

Key points from the interview

- Enjoy the journey more than the destination.
- Balance mental wellbeing, good food, sleep, regular exercise
- Give and receive support from your family and friends
- Relax and don't stress about small issues
- Importance of understanding your customer's customers
- Importance of perseverance through difficulties that we all face

Robert (Ramin) Roshan

Founder and CEO of Byte, a successful medium-sized IT Consultancy.

From a refugee to creating a successful digital technology company from scratch. A well - balanced Entrepreneur. *"Don't sweat the small stuff."*

Further information

- *https://byte.com.au/*

Category

Technical entrepreneur. A technical entrepreneur uses technology as a base to add other management skills including sales and marketing to build a business

I. KEY DATES

- Ramin (who later changed to Robert after arriving in Australia) was born in Iran.
- In 1985 he came to Australia with his older brother. Although their plane arrived in Perth in the middle of the night, many people had gathered to greet them. Their friendly faces made a positive and lasting impression. The people at the airport were mostly the new refugee arrivals and their friends. At the time most of the refugees from Iran were young.
- After nine months in Perth, Robert moved to Melbourne, where he studied computer science and electronics.
- In the early 1990s, Robert worked for Bonlac Food before branching out on his own as an entrepreneur. His strong will and his perfectionism, which he admits may have made him difficult to manage as an employee, proved beneficial when it came to starting a business.
- In 1993 Robert founded Byte: "the business was just me". The business started with humble beginnings in a backroom in a house in Kew with a single three-day contract.
- In 1999 Byte had its first major contract with Amcor and did a lot of Y2K work.

Authors' note: remember the Y2K drama?

- In early 2000 Byte diversified in e-commerce as it was the "dot com" era! It was a significant focus on supply chain projects.
- The Global Financial Crisis of late 2000 made Byte move from only performing project work to doing project work, and managed services and recurring revenue work.
- In 2016 Robert appointed a good friend and mentor Greg Embleton as CEO, and brought Stanley Havea on board as Sales and Executive Director. This allowed the company to expand into both Sydney and Canberra. It also meant that Robert could spend more quality time with his family.
- Today:
    - the company employs more than 100 people, with offices in Melbourne, Sydney and Canberra.
    - Byte is a leading digital technology provider, partnering with Telstra, Microsoft, CISCO and Citrix.
    - Byte's success has meant it can offer internships, do pro-bono work and donate to charity.
    - Robert recognises that the persecution he experienced as a member of the Baha'i faith in Iran is impossible to forget, it also allowed him the opportunity to come to Australia and start a family. He has fond memories of growing up in Esfahan, a city he likens to Melbourne, but Australia is home and has been for a long time.

II. GETTING TO KNOW THE PERSON

1. What is success?

Robert says that to be truly successful people need to be authentic and strive to be the best version of themselves. He defines success as 'the building and sharing of things', and that the important part of this is 'the Journey rather than the destination'. He applies this philosophy to both his business and personal life, as he considers that both require an investment in time and effort.

Those who know Robert understand how important family is to him. He has been married to his wife Ruth, artist and musician, for longer than he has been at the helm of Byte. All of Robert's extended family now lives in Australia. He says: "It is a big family, as I have four brothers and one sister and their partners and children, about 20 of us in total. I love to spend time with my dad, who is 85 now." Robert's dad loves a game of backgammon. When Robert asks his dad how he is, he always says, "I couldn't be better!" Robert must have inherited some of his optimism, because he says: "No one lives forever and I'm old enough to avoid regrets". He says that "Family and work are the competing priorities you need to juggle when time is the most valuable commodity."

Robert tries hard to deliver on all his commitments to his family which includes the Byte family. He considers that happiness is achieved by reaching your potential and purpose in life, which includes the spiritual, family, and work dimensions. He also includes in this recipe a dose of exercise to keep "all this perpetual motion going."

2. What is your favourite TV show, movie or book and why?

- Books:
  - *Man's search for meaning* by Victor Frankl, which is a study of a Holocaust survivor and hope for survival.
  - *Creating a new mind* by Paul Lample. This is a Baha'i text
- Movie: *Blade Runner* (Original preferred)
- TV: *Deadwood.* This is an American western television series.

3. What are your hobbies and/or Interests?

Robert is quite active, and he is especially keen on skiing and cycling. He considers himself a "new age guy" and loves cooking while his wife does the house repairs and maintenance.

III. TIPS

4. How did you get through your worst times?

Robert emphasises the need for perspective. He considers that most of our day-to-day problems are relatively minor and unlikely to impact on the most important aspects of life, that is the health and well-being of family. For Robert, even the most serious business problems rate only 6 out of 10, allowing him "to keep calm". He does not panic and carefully collects the information before making any decisions.

Robert is keen on listening to classical music in the evenings, this along with his cycling passion help keep him relaxed.

5. What keeps you awake at night?

Robert realises that there are some problems that he cannot do anything about – such as health issues and family matters. In the case of business, he says that if you are staying awake at night after 25 years in business, perhaps you should consider other ways of earning a dollar! He believes that sleep is essential, because interrupted sleep is likely to induce errors during the day.

6. What are your typical daily routines?

Robert has a weekly routine rather than a daily routine and aims for the routine to include flexibility. His weekly routine includes:

- Ensuring that at least 4 days of every week he cycles, and for this he usually rises at 6 am.
- Cooking three days of every week for the family.
- Maintaining his diary at a maximum of 60% full.
- Retiring by 10.30 to 11 pm, and winds down by listening or watching something interesting yet peaceful.
- Visiting his dad to have one-on-one time, including playing backgammon.

7. What advice would you give yourself starting out?

Figure 25 - A relaxed Robert Roshan

Robert would advise young people not to get too stressed about business issues and to put life into perspective. He considers that in his area of IT, it is unlikely anyone will die due to any mistake. Also, he says that young people should enjoy the journey rather than focus on the outcome. He feels that there needs to be a balance between the required motivation to create a sense of urgency, but not to create unnecessary stressful situations. He noted that many people need to create a certain edge to perform well.

Authors' note: think of John McEnroe, the highly successful 1970s, 1980s and 1990s American tennis player that used creating disruption as a competitive advantage).

IV. BUSINESS CASE EXAMPLES

8. Provide a case you managed well and why?

In 1998, Byte's first major contract was with AMCOR (now Orora Group). Today the packaging company remains one of Byte's valued customers. Robert advises that the key to success is to understand the client's business and their priorities. He feels that many people do not understand the need for an end-to-end viewpoint of their clients' business. Robert says it is essential for him to realise that his customers' priority is their customers. Therefore, he needs to understand his customers' customers.

9. Provide a case that did not go well and why?

Byte was born in 1993, and the company grew quickly. He feels that in some ways, it grew too quickly. He recalls that within five years, it employed 40 people. "That was the result of Byte acquiring a company for a seven-figure sum," says Robert. "Two years later, the only asset that was left of that company was a "lava" lamp that Robert kept at home which he now jokes about.

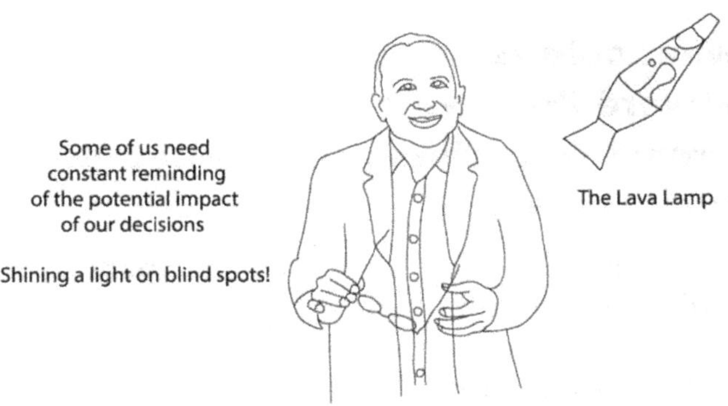

Figure 26 - Robert and the infamous lava lamp

It would take Byte five years to recover, but Robert took the long view and at the end of the day, it was 'only money'. He adjusted his lifestyle, changed his plans, and moved on. "You have to," as he says. "You must accept that out of 10 decisions you make, 2 of them will not be good decisions." He laughs and continues. "Unfortunately, this was an important decision, and it went wrong." Robert says there will always be decisions which in hindsight were not great. However, it is a test to deal with the situation once it becomes evident that there is a problem. He feels that many people do not have the mental and physical fitness required to navigate their way out of these difficulties.

10. What conclusions can be drawn by comparing these cases?

The failure of the acquisition was a test of Robert's resilience. He says that in business, you need a strong resolve and that it is important to view mistakes simply as obstacles that need to be overcome, or as opportunities to learn. He feels, and quotes "that if you do not have that mindset, I think you're going to have a very tough time." On reflection, Robert says self-belief was critical to his ability to move forward. He credits this to the love of his family and the support he received from the Australian people when he first arrived here. That support has given him the confidence to face many challenges.

11. What cultural issues did you experience? How were they overcome? How is Australia different? Were these cases affected by cultural issues?

Robert grew up in the minority Baha'i faith in Iran. Because of this life was difficult, and he had to deal with a lot of prejudice. He built up grit and strength to deal with these challenges. Some people still have some prejudices, which he finds disappointing, but he treats everyone the same. He came to Australia as a 20-year-old and married at 25 to an Australian and has never had any major difficulty with the Australian culture. He does understand that sometimes you need to address people from different cultures differently. At Byte, there is a significant emphasis on the culture of the organisation and management team to treat everyone the same, and this includes the team in India.

Authors' note: Compare Robert's view of his Indian staff to that of the Warrier case study, being Case Study Number 1.

Byte makes a conscious choice to employ people of all ages and nationalities, including those that find it difficult to get employment due to their level of language skills. When receiving their resumes, Robert feels a deep empathy with such people. "When I came to

Australia, I could not speak English. You realise that their intellect is perfect as they have done all the training, but they cannot communicate well. Nevertheless, that doesn't mean they shouldn't have a job." Robert says that he has learnt to employ people based on character. He has a soft spot for employing people with English as their second language.

Inclusivity and investing in people are two of Byte's values. Accordingly, Byte strives to integrate religious and cultural practices into the working day, to ensure employees feel at home. It is not unusual for Byte's Melbourne meeting room to be turned into a prayer room.

V. VOLATILITY (FOR EXAMPLE COVID)

12. How has the virus affected your business?

Robert sees the COVID-19 pandemic has impacted him, his staff and the business in the following areas:

- Physical well-being
- Mental well-being
- Customer service delivery
- Financial impact/unpredictable nature.

The JobKeeper government COVID-19 payments were of some minor assistance for the company, but his staff are highly paid, so the JobKeeper rate is low in proportion. He stated that the business lost 60% of its project-based work, but lost only 20% in the managed services area of the business. It was lucky that the Byte business has a significant managed services revenue and good customer base to help them navigate through the pandemic.

13. What lasting impact do you think it will have on your business?

One impact is the importance of *working on the business than in the business*, for example the need to take time to focus more on risk management.

Robert has emphasised the long-term importance of strong mental and physical well-being, particularly with staff working from home. He noted that currently less than 60% of his staff are working in the office and that many of those coming into the office are not keen on public transport.

Robert has recently moved the office from St Kilda Road (the inner city of Melbourne) to the CBD as the St Kilda Road landlord was not co-operative and flexible for Byte's needs.

One problem with working from home is the loss of productivity from the collaborative nature of face-to-face working. He feels that whilst individuals can work from home, there is better work productivity when working physically together.

14. What have you learned from it that you will now implement in your business?

Robert feels that there are many lessons to be learnt from the COVID-19 pandemic, and some of these changes will most likely be permanent. He sees that an emphasis on the managed service part of the business, perhaps comprising some 50% to 70% of the business, will provide more stability against these potential interruptions. It is his opinion that COVID-19 has been a real test of grit in management, that is the ability to grind positively through difficult times, but there will always be a level of unpredictability. Management needs to be able to quickly react to issues that arise. He feels that it is now more important than ever to regularly have his Risk and Compliance Committee meet and keep the risk register up to date. Planning for a pandemic, and like situations, should be a permanent feature from this. Robert said he had previously implemented this process when working on a consultancy project with the Accountancy firm, Pitcher Partners.

> **Authors' note:** COVID-19 reminds us of the need to try to identify volatility in advance and seek to manage the identified risk.

VI. FAMILY BUSINESS

15. Are you in a family business and from your experience what do you think are the advantages and disadvantages of family working in the business?

Robert does not consider Byte to be a family business, as he is the sole owner and decision maker.

The success of a family business depends on the style of business management. Robert says that his business often requires robust discussions, and this can affect personal relationships causing collateral damage. He generally prefers not to work with family members because of the potential for this damage to personal relationships. Robert would like to ensure his family relationships are as harmonious as possible.

The success of families working together also may depend on the nature of the business, where some businesses may be more amenable to family members working together. His business is in professional services which necessarily need to be very dynamic and pro-active to customer needs. He feels that this can easily be disrupted unless the right services are delivered promptly.

He concluded by stating that risks increase when one adds the dynamics of a family member working in the business. Robert advises that he can handle this increased risk, as he has employed family in the past, but it may not be for everyone.

Figure 27 - The Byte Head Office team Robert is just to the right of the middle wearing glasses, grey jacket and white shirt

FUN FACTS ON: COMPUTERS AND THE INTERNET

Computers

- *"I think there is a world market for about five computers."*, Thomas **J Watson founder IBM**
- *"There is no reason for any individual to have a computer in his home."*, **Ken Olsen, president of Digital Equipment Corporation.**
- *"Never trust a computer you can't throw out a window."*, **Steve Wozniak**
- *"The good news about computers is that they do what you tell them to do. The bad news is that they do what you tell them to do."*, **Ted Nelson**
-

Internet

- *"The truth is no online database will replace your daily newspaper"*, **Clifford Stoll**. 1995 Newspaper article entitled 'The Internet? Bah!'

Margaret Harmer OAM

From a mother losing a child to the co-founder of a not- for- profit organisation helping bereaved families

INTRODUCTION

Key points from the interview

- The power of sharing your experience with someone that has also had been "through it", called "the lived experience", and also known as mutual self-help or "peer support"
- Importance of taking some time out to avoid burn-out.
- Find someone that can be a regular advisor or mentor.
- Hire a good publicist/marketer for your business, as in the long term they may be one of your most important advisers.
- Plan for future succession and a smooth transition.

Margaret Harmer OAM

Margaret is a Melbourne social entrepreneur and the founder of The Compassionate Friends (TCF), a Not-for-Profit organisation, and a pioneer entrepreneur of the "Mutual Self Help" concept. Her personal mantra is "from those to whom much is given, much will be required", this is the motto of Dr Wood, her former school principal at Methodist Ladies College.

Further information

- *https://tcfa.org.au/about-us/* (includes links to State organisations)

Category

Social entrepreneur. *A person who pursues novel applications that have the potential to solve community-based problems. These individuals are willing to take on the risk and effort to create positive changes in society through their initiatives. According to Investopedia (2021b) social entrepreneurs may believe that this practice is a way to connect you to your life's purpose, help others find theirs, and make a difference in the world (all while eking out a living).*

I. KEY DATES

- In 1950 Margaret at age 16 met Lindsay Harmer (21) a final year Pharmacy student from Shepparton, Victoria.
- In her matriculation year Margaret's father was transferred from Perth to Melbourne and she found it hard to start anew.
- Her father did not encourage her to attend University, which she had wanted to do.
- After completing a business course, she became secretary to the general manager of *The Sun* news pictorial newspaper and later was secretary to one of the *Herald and Weekly Times* editors.
- In 1954 Margaret married Lindsay and before the age of 28 they had three lovely children Rosalind, Wendy and Rhys.

- In 1973 extreme sadness came into their lives when Lindsay, Margaret and Rhys (11) were involved in a car accident caused by an intoxicated speeding driver. Rhys was killed and Margaret seriously injured. Lindsay carried mental wounds due to the extreme tragedy of the situation, called Post-Traumatic Stress Disorder (PTSD).
- In 1978 Margaret and Lindsay founded The Compassionate Friends (TCF) organisation from the lounge room of their home in Glen Waverley. Lindsay was the Director and Margaret was President and they promoted the organisation on the relatively new concept of mutual support (self-help) for bereaved families. From the start it became a source of comfort for many where they could find support. In 1979 they brought out the International TCF founder, Rev. Dr Simon Stephens from the UK, and Margaret and he travelled to New South Wales and South Australia together and appeared on television. Margaret and Lindsay later travelled to country towns, and TCF chapters started throughout all states.
- In 1981 Margaret travelled to Western Australia and initiated the first meeting in Perth.
- In 1982 Margaret and Lindsay were able to set up the first Bereaved Parent Drop-In Centre in the world in Syndal, Victoria.
- In March 1991 Margaret and Lindsay stepped back from their managerial positions in TCF to allow others to take over and transition to the next stage. They were aware of "Founders Syndrome" and did not interfere in future decisions and management.

Authors' note: Founders syndrome is the tendency of founders to constrain other people's ideas with their own

- In 2016 Margaret and Lindsay were each awarded the OAM (medal of the Order of Australia in the Queen's Birthday Honours.)
- In 2019, Lindsay died aged 90 after several years of suffering from Parkinson's disease and other illnesses.

- In 2021 she was made Co-Patron of The Compassionate Friends.
- Recent years: Margaret was involved in a range of activities within the community. See the list of hobbies and interests in Questions 2 and 3, below.

II. GETTING TO KNOW THE PERSON

1. What is success?

Margaret sees success as being able to have a meaningful life of contribution, especially with the support of a happy family life. She feels fortunate to have had enough resources to live reasonably well, and which enabled her to give of herself to community work. Margaret feels it is ironic that had she gone to University rather than listen to her father, she may not have been able to devote herself to the community work which she believes was her life's purpose.

2. What is your favourite TV show, movie or book and why?

- Television and film: Margaret likes television news and discussion about the news such as *Insiders*, *Four corners*, *Australian Story*, etc. She mainly watches SBS and ABC and loves historical and thoughtful shows like *Compass*, good movies, Netflix. Programs like *Downton Abbey* and comedies like *Seinfeld.*
- Books: Since her childhood Margaret has been an avid reader and reads most types including thoughtful, crime, historical, romance, family sagas etc. Recently she has read *Any ordinary day* by Leigh Sales, *Brooklyn* by Colm Toibin and *American Dirt* by Jeanine Cummins.

3. What are your hobbies and/or Interests?

At age 88, her family is her main interest these days with seven grandchildren and their partners plus almost twelve great grandchildren. Her elder daughter Rosalind died from cancer 6 years ago leaving three adult children with families. Margaret is very involved with her whole family now and finds them very supportive and interesting. Her main support is her remaining special child of three, Wendy.

Due to disability, Margaret has a limited range of interests now but in the past, she was very involved with:

- Probus (a group focusing on fun, friendship and fellowship in retirement) and her friends in that group.
- Ancestry discoveries.
- St. Michael's Uniting Church in Melbourne and Psychology lectures from Dr. Francis Macnab.
- Lifeline counselling on the phones and Save the Children Fund.
- She enjoyed surfing and beach days in summer.

She is not particularly interested in watching sport, except tennis finals and the Olympics.

III. TIPS

4. How did you get through your worst times?

Margaret's life with Lindsay, a pharmacist for 30 years in Glen Waverley, and with her family was once very enjoyable, successful and happy. Just after a long-awaited purchase of a beach house the car accident happened. Margaret herself was seriously injured. Lindsay after trying to cope with the accident scene, the death of Rhys and Margaret's predicament was for some time badly affected by post-traumatic stress disorder (PTSD). He found it hard to return to operating the pharmacy but did so. They struggled on for the sake of their children. Their daughter, Rosalind had her VCE exams 2 weeks after the accident. In the time following the accident they looked desperately for help and support. They tried various doctors and therapists but could not find anyone on their "wave length". Good hearted family and friends tried but seemed unable to help. The churches didn't seem to strike the right chord either.

Margaret and Lindsay didn't know anyone else that had lost a child and they felt very alone. In her loneliness, Margaret began to work for Lifeline (a charity providing 24/7 crisis support and suicide prevention services) as a telephone counsellor and found some friends there. Slowly the idea formed of the benefit of mutual (lived experience) assistance from people who has also gone through similar tragedies. This slow transformation got them through the worst of times. In later years, Margaret says they were always so relieved to see others similarly move on from extreme grief to being able to live again with TCF assistance.

5. What keeps you awake at night?

In addition to being worried about TCF and various bereaved parents Margaret was always worried about Lindsay, who had post-traumatic stress and various serious health problems for many years before he died in 2019. She advises that those were very stressful days. Their grief and resulting stress caused difficulties in getting peaceful sleep. However, fortunately these days she is much more relaxed about life, except for the usual aches and pains of older age.

6. What are your typical daily routines?

This was really dependant on the stage of life. Margaret is not particularly structured in terms of routines now but of course when the children were young and needed school transport, meals etc, a certain amount of routine was necessary. Lindsay always lived a totally structured life with the pharmacy to run. In those days Margaret would regularly go into the Pharmacy part time to do the banking, accounts and other work as needed. Lindsay would open the pharmacy about 8.30am and not be home until 6.30pm. These days Margaret rises about 8.30 and occasionally goes out, but not much these days and she no longer drives.

7. What advice would you give yourself starting out?

Margaret noted that to build the TCF organisation from scratch and to achieve its success it required the full and often overwhelming commitment of both herself and Lindsay. Margaret and Lindsay had complementary skills which worked well together. She does feel that in retrospect perhaps if they had taken more time off on a regular basis, they may have had a more balanced life. Looking back, it would have been helpful to have had a mentor, but she and Lindsay may not have accepted their advice. They probably would have only listened to another bereaved parent.

IV. BUSINESS CASE EXAMPLES

8. Provide a case you managed well and why?

TCF was, in a sense, impetuously started. One night in 1978 she read the Herald newspaper and saw a small article about the Compassionate Friends in New York offering self-help for bereaved parents. Margaret says she and Lindsay then immediately knew this was to be their life's passion. They hunted down the journalist who said that she would do an article for the new Melbourne start-up group but only after it commenced. Margaret advertised in the local paper for the new group and immediately people started coming to their home in Glen Waverly in response. The Journalist was true to her word and about three months later published a full-page article. This obviously tapped into a desperate need because they were inundated with bereaved families from then on. They then tracked down the English founder of TCF, Reverend Dr Simon Stephens (not easy in pre-internet days) and brought him out to Australia the following year to help publicise TCF throughout Australia.

Figure 28 - Rev Dr Simon Stephens, Margaret and Lindsay Harmer - 2013

Before Reverend Simon's visit they hired a publicist for a few weeks to make bookings for Simon including appearing with Margaret on various popular TV and radio programmes. They used this publicity to reach like-minded people in other states to explain the needs of bereaved parents.

For the first few years Lindsay ran the pharmacy business by day and worked for TCF at nights and weekends. Margaret spent most days doing TCF work including phone counselling, visiting parents and all the secretarial work. They both did a great deal of public speaking.

They continued holding regular meetings for bereaved parents at home but as they spread the concept and their work received considerable media publicity, the numbers grew rapidly, and they started to convene monthly 'Friendship Nights' in a large city hall they hired. They began writing, preparing and funding the post-out of a regular newsletter to bereaved parents throughout Australia, which so many parents acknowledged was like 'raindrops on parched soil'.

As demand and need increased rapidly, Lindsay decided to close their long running, successful family pharmacy in 1981 so that he could devote himself to TCF and bereaved parents. They urgently set about obtaining Government funding to open an office outside their home and Margaret in particular worked assiduously at the task of grant applications. Margaret brought her past high level professional secretarial skills and her experience as a past president and secretary of community organisations including "Save the Children" Mt Waverley to these roles.

The first Bereaved Parents' Drop-in Centre in Australia (and the world) was subsequently opened in 1982 in Blackburn Road, Mt Waverley. Other places had offices but not drop-in centres. The first government funding of $7,000 was used to pay for the rental of a five-room apartment, utility services and for a part-time secretary.

About two years later a further grant was made to offer a small salary for Lindsay, obtain some equipment, pay postage and purchase library books and tapes for the library which was now in great demand. In addition to phone counselling and meetings with bereaved parents who called at the Centre, they wrote literally thousands of personal letters to bereaved parents all over Australia;

all tailored to individual needs and also provided literature and tapes. Remember that there were no computers or email then.

Figure 29 - Margaret and Lindsay Harmer at the Syndal drop-in centre 1982

As well as "friendship days" (and the "friendship nights" which were held in the city of Melbourne) some of the most successful innovations for the use of the centre were the holding of monthly individual special needs groups for parents of children who had experienced sudden deaths, illnesses, suicide, murder, baby deaths. Also held were men's groups and social and "getting well" days featuring lunches, craft, cookery, film, music, fashion etc. The centre was used extensively.

TCF in the USA was a great source of support and benefit to both the Margaret and Lindsay and TCF, and ultimately, they attended four inspiring conferences over the years at their own expense.

Today most Governments recognise the effective cost-benefit of these organisations that actually save it money by the use of volunteer peer support.

9. Provide a case that did not go well and why?

Case 1 - Loss of Funding

During the economic recession of 1990-1991, along with many other charities, TCF suddenly lost their Government funding of approximately $72,000 per annum. This sadly resulted in them having to close the busy Syndal drop-in centre, known to members as their "oasis". This tremendous disruption meant that all equipment and furniture had to be moved to Margaret and Lindsay's home. They even had to have the photocopier at the end of their bed! This was an incredibly painful and difficult time when it was felt that all the gains seem to have been lost. Groups and meetings ceased and only the telephone caring remained.

Margaret then invited a Health Department official to visit who was shown the complete disarray of TCF files and equipment within her disordered home. Margaret lobbied the Government to simply fund a basic rental for a hall in Camberwell and promised to staff it with volunteers and paying all costs themselves. This offer was accepted and in March 1991 they moved to Camberwell and the recovery from this point was slow but ultimately successful.

Case 2 – The path to peer support policies and procedures

Along the way to establish mutual self-help there were some hard lessons to learn. One example she remembers was in one support group that she hosted; one person went too far in detailing gruesome details. As a result, the others in the group did not come back. Margaret realised the importance of establishing proper procedures and policies for TCF, including tactics for handling difficult situations.

Two other difficult situations come to mind: The first is that the Victorian Chief Psychiatrist requested Margaret to assist a mother in prison who had after murdered her two children. Margaret agreed to do this although it was outside of her peer support role and one which should have required a trained professional. Margaret did visit her in prison for some months and they related well but was advised not to continue by a local church minister and Margaret's family who felt it was not her role. She was also contacted continually by the grieving prisoner's mother. The second difficult situation was coping with the volume of new members wanting to drop into their home and contact the Harmers at all times (including a long call during Christmas dinner). It became like having a Lifeline (a charitable crisis support centre) at home. One bereaved mother came every morning at 8.15 am!

10. What conclusions can be drawn by comparing these cases?

The Harmer's efforts, determination and entrepreneurial skills helped establish, run and expand the organisation. However, as has been seen it was often difficult to balance their family life with that of operating and expanding TCF.

11. What cultural issues did you experience? How were they overcome? How is Australia different? Were these cases affected by.

Margaret and Lindsay also invited an English social worker to stay with them (amongst many people who stayed over the years). The social worker remarked "where are all the Aboriginal people?" Margaret noted that in the community in which they mixed there were indeed very few Aboriginals. When attending USA conferences in the 80's, she also noted only two black people were present. Margaret emphasizes that TCF has always been open to all races and religions. The TCF organisation worldwide is non-denominational. She advises that she has never witnessed any cross-cultural problems or issues.

V. VOLATILITY (FOR EXAMPLE COVID)

12. How has the virus affected your business?

As Margaret is fully retired, the COVID lockdown did not have that much of an impact on her, although she has followed the discussions in the media and felt it was a good time for reflection on what is important in life. Margaret has followed the impact on TCF members and was impressed at the innovative ways that the organisation responded with on-line support groups and the 24-hour support line.

13. What lasting impact do you think it will have on your business?

Margaret thinks TCF will need to continue to monitor their resources to cope in the future especially with regard to future government funding.

14. What have you learned from it that you will now implement in your business?

As mentioned in Question 13, it is flexibility, resources and risk management have now become integral in TCF.

VI. FAMILY BUSINESS

15. Are you in a family business and from your experience what do you think are the advantages and disadvantages of family working in the business?

In the early stages it looked like a family business with Margaret and Lindsay. It is an interesting question for TCF because it is not a family business as we see in the corner grocery employing family members, but on the other hand TCF members see the organisation as a community, an "Oasis" that for many becomes their pseudo-family support.

Figure 30 - Margaret and Lindsay Harmer (dec.) in 2009

FUN FACTS ON: LIFESTYLE ETC

Lifestyle

No more coffee and tea. In 1937, **Nikola Tesla** predicted that by 2020 people will no longer drink anything that will poison the body with harmful ingredients.

Smoking

"If excessive smoking actually plays a role in the production of lung cancer it seems to be a minor one", said **W.C. Heuper**, the director of the National Cancer Institute's Environmental Cancer Section, in 1954. Whoops.

Future

"The best thing about the future is that it comes one day at a time.", **Abraham Lincoln**

Other

"The difference between stupidity and genius is that genius has its limits.", **Albert Einstein**

"If slaughterhouses had glass walls, everyone would be a vegetarian.", **Paul McCartney**

(Disclosure – one of the Authors is a vegetarian)

Matija Squire

From teenage mother without schooling to a double graduate and successful business adviser.

INTRODUCTION

Key points from the interview

- Your circumstances should never dictate your potential
- Don't be afraid of talking to anyone and understanding that everyone is human
- Focus on what you can control and accept what you can't
- Understanding the people you are dealing with as "everything is about people" rather than the product or Industry

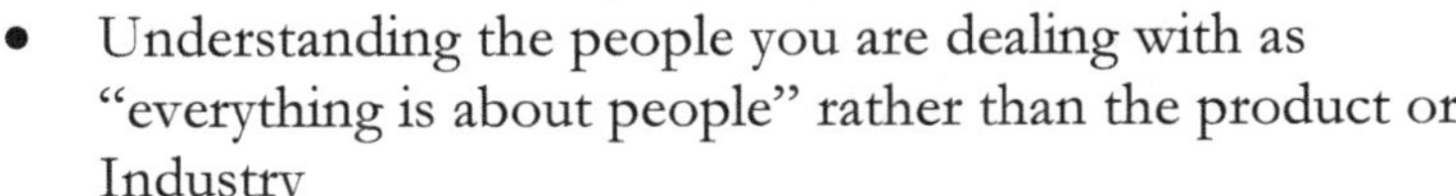

Matija Squire

Matija had a difficult beginning: motherhood at 17 and then feeling that she had no life ahead of her. She thought about her future and decided to take some risks in order to better her life. Her risks succeeded: she evolved into a talented sought-after entrepreneur and adviser to entrepreneurs. Matija's primary role is in consulting with start-ups and coordinating with them to obtain finance and equity funding from venture capital. Her motto is "your circumstances should never dictate your potential".

Further information

- *https://www.theparadigmeffect.com.au/*
- *https://www.theparadigmeffect.com.au/about*

Category

Entrepreneurial consultant: Consulting on Start-up finance, Executive coaching, team culture, recruitment, Culture Mapping.

I. KEY DATES

- 2008-2012
    - Matija grew up Broken Hill, a small New South Wales country town, left high school early as a young mother with family problems.
    - She continuously worked since age 14 in various part time jobs to support herself.
- 2013
    - She attended the James Cook University Open Day in Townsville and discovered an alternate pathway into university and decided to pursue her education and against all odds completed a dual degree in Arts–Business.
    - She undertook part of her studies in Japan.
    - Fast forward to now, and Matija today is an accomplished lecturer, speaker, business owner, board director and start-up mentor, who found a new way forward for her family (she, her son and husband) through the life-changing gateway of education.

  - Matija often mentors at the grass roots start-ups level, providing tools and education to enable start-ups to enter global markets and successfully raise funds.
  - She has lectured at tertiary institutions since 2015.
  - Matija launched her first start-up in 2017, which specialised in branding and marketing, working with global companies such as Cisco.
  - She is passionate about providing opportunities for people to create solutions that will contribute to global prosperity and has completed start-up programs hosted by University of Central London, Ritsumeikan Asia Pacific University in Japan, James Cook University in Townsville, Queensland and the University of New England in Northern New South Wales.
- 2016
  - First place recipient of Google Start-Up Weekend at James Cook University
  - Living in Japan, she completed the University of Central London's Entrepreneurship for Global Prosperity program at Ritsumeikan Asia Pacific University Japan
  - Completed her Business Scholarship in Japan.
  - December – moved to Sydney
- 2017
  - Started the early genesis of her consulting business whilst working.
- 2018
  - Launched LinkedIn content, which gained the attention of large companies such as Cisco, built an audience of over 20,000
  - March - Invited as a guest to attend Cisco Live, met the Vice President of Cisco Michelle Dennedy who encouraged her to start her own company.
  - July - launched her own company "The Paradigm Effect", joined the Sydney Start-up Hub as a member and mentor, assisting start-ups with marketing and personal branding

- 2019
  - Launched InBestThing and joined the board of the Australia Philippines Business Council
  - Hosted the first ever Philippine/Australia Start-up showcase in collaboration with the Philippines government (Filipinovation)
  - Was invited to be a community partner in the first Philippines Start-up Week in Manila
  - Launched the Philippines Culture Study
  - Delivered programs and workshops internationally to assist Filipino start-ups
  - Hosted the Vice President of the Philippines Leni Robredo
  - Hosted the Australian Ambassador the Philippines the Honourable Stephen Robertson.
  - Attended the CEO Round table at Ernst and Young to discuss trade and investment opportunities between Australia and Philippines.
  - Joined Universal Business School Sydney (UBSS) as a Fellow
  - Hosted a panel for the United Nations Sustainable Development Goals
- 2020
  - Completed training in Fingerprint for Success People analytics software used by the likes of Atlassian and Canva
  - Guest speaker for the Asia-Berlin Start-up Summit
  - As a Director of the APBC, contributed to raising over $70,000 in funds for Filipino students in Australia affected by COVID-19
  - Acted as interim COO for an online education company
  - Provided over 40 hours of pro bono consulting for start-ups during the covid lockdown
- Now
  - Matija travelled to Japan regularly, approximately twice per year for the last 6 years (COVID pandemic excluded)
  - Matija's role is acting as a middle person between Venture Capitalists (VCs) and start-up businesses. The focus is always on the people rather than the

product as the skills and attitudes of the people are the key ingredient. Matija is involved in is "scale-ups" and as well start-ups

II. GETTING TO KNOW THE PERSON

1. What is success?

Matija says for some people success may be framed in financial terms. For her, success is about alignment of her work to her values and achieving a sense of belonging to her family and business community.

2. What is your favourite TV show, movie or book and why?

- Books:
  - Fiction – Brandon Sanderson, an American author of epic fantasy and science fiction.
  - Non-Fiction – David Goleman who has written books about Emotional Intelligence.
- TV:
  - Various Netflix movies.
- Favourite movie:
  - *Howl's Moving Castle* (Which is a Japanese animated fantasy. Japanese is Matija's second language).

3. What are your hobbies and/or Interests?

Matija is fan of pop-culture and engaging in her creative side. She is a collector of retro and rare games and is a member of a local dance studio where she learns hip-hop with her son.

She finds that taking regular breaks to do these activities assists her concentration in her work.

Figure 31 - Matija gaming with her son

III. TIPS

4. How did you get through your worst times?

Matija says that she found becoming self-aware of her potential was the key to working through difficult times. An example of this was her first, and very stressful, day at University. Once she gave herself permission to believe in herself that she had the potential to study she soon relaxed. Remember Matija's motto, *"your circumstances should never dictate your potential."*

5. What keeps you awake at night?

Matija says she tends to over-think, wanting to do everything at once and is often in "overdrive". This can be a problem at night, so she practices calm by reading or listening to music in order to get to sleep.

6. What are your typical daily routines?

Outside of certain constraints, for example taking her son to school, Matija likes to have as flexible work schedule as possible. She blocks out time for breaks but overall, she does not have strict routines. A daily coffee is, however, a required standard morning habit.

7. What advice would you give yourself starting out?

Matija says not to be afraid of talking to anyone and understanding that everyone is human. She was at a conference with a top company Chief Executive Officer (CEO), and they ended up exchanging photos of their pets, and casually talking about their lives, it was a reminder that we are more similar than different. Matija's father gave her some advice when she was young which turned her life around, which was that it was up to Matija to make her own decisions in life, and he would support her in whatever she chose. She understands the importance of self-empowerment and supporting young people to own their own decisions and make something of it.

IV. BUSINESS CASE EXAMPLES

8. Provide a case you managed well and why?

Matija was in Japan for studies and became involved in negotiating a dispute for some Australians. She was able to help resolve the problem as she was able to speak Japanese and understand the Japanese culture.

9. Provide a case that did not go well and why?

Case 1

Matija was offered a project in the Philippines just as the COVID-19 pandemic hit. She was considering this project but realised the downside risk that she could have been stuck in the Philippines and locked out of coming back to Australia. Despite it being a short project, she chose not to take the risk. She was unable to do this project from Australia on-line as the Philippines, like the Japanese, prefer face-to-face project delivery.

Case 2

Matija was working with a start-up and was offered the opportunity to join in as co-founder which would have involved her in a long-term working relationship as well as an investor. She opted to delay this decision to experience if this company was the right fit. The business had considerable potential, due to this she ignored the early warning signs that there was a contradiction on the values and actions of the company. Ultimately, once she was able to acknowledge the reality, she realised it went against her personal values and she negotiated her exit. Had she not ignored the early warning flags, she could have limited the stress caused by working in an environment that was not congruent with her values.

10. What conclusions can be drawn by comparing these cases?

Case 1

Matija emphasises the need to understand the people you are dealing with as "everything is about people" rather than the product or Industry. In Japanese culture you need to be there in person unlike say in the USA or even in Singapore where they are happy to work on-line.

Authors' note: Compare this to Greg Whateley's interview 7 which also discusses this specific point.

Matija now ensures that wherever she works a high priority is placed on the ability to get back to her family quickly.

Case 2

Matija said that it is part of her normal work to consult in cases of differences in values that cause friction. Ironically, she found herself not being able to be fully objective when dealing with a co-founder in a new business.

Figure 32 - Matija at Fishburnes in the Sydney Start-up Hub

11. What cultural issues did you experience? How were they overcome? How is Australia different? Were these cases affected by.

Matija responded as follows:

- *Attitudes to On-Line work*: Matija has experienced the different cultural attitudes to working on-line versus face to face. This has had an impact on her work. As stated in Part A of Question 9 Matija was not able to complete the Philippines job due to her client's reluctance on using on-line communication (for example Zoom or TEAMS). Instead, she is currently working on analysing and mapping a company's alignment of values and testing them with evidence which she can mainly do on-line from Australia. Matija's preferred method of working is to collect all her data first and then analyse it. Due to the on-line nature of the work, she has had to compromise on her own personal "culture" and work on an incremental basis, that is work on a greater volume of smaller sets of data.

- *Nonverbal clues*: In Japan she became aware of the cultural non-verbal clues such facial expression, tone of voice, posture etc. Matija watches these carefully to check whether she is properly understanding the message. In some Japanese circumstances email is the preferred method of communication. They use a formal structure of speech known as "keigo" to avoid misunderstandings. Matija notes that it is interesting how different cultures have their own nuances for example when communicating in Japan the Japanese always talk about the weather first.

V. VOLATILITY (FOR EXAMPLE COVID)

12. How has the virus affected your business?

Matija prefers to see volatility as "uncertainty" as the two go hand in hand. She thinks many people are either resistant to change or are accepting of change and therefore fairly adaptable. She sees herself as a very adaptable person.

Authors' note: perhaps the way she sees herself is a result of her early life experiences.

She did lose some business due to the pandemic but has replaced this with consulting.

13. What lasting impact do you think it will have on your business?

Matija believes there will be more uncertainty in the business for the foreseeable future and any new contract will need to allow for this. There will not be as much consistency in delivering projects and there will need to be an allowance for external circumstances. All her clients are from personal referrals, and she has never been out of work. She is used to having to work 7 days but at the moment she has a much lower level of work, which is not a bad thing. She currently is working on one large corporate project, one small start-up and one mentoring project.

14. What have you learned from it that you will now implement in your business?

Matija will now allow for more uncertainty. She understands that not everything can be achieved and sometimes she must accept a less than optimal result due to things outside of her control. It is what she learns from the experience and how she can improve that she places most importance on. Matija said she now focuses on what she can control and accepting of those things she can't control.

Authors' note: if more people thought like this people would have less stress.

VI. FAMILY BUSINESS

15. Are you in a family business and from your experience what do you think are the advantages and disadvantages of family working in the business?

Matija does not see her business as a family business. She likes to separate business and family and does not identify as a "mumtrepreneur" (a woman who combines running a business

Figure 33 - Matija on graduation day with her son

enterprise with looking after her children). She is, however, happy for others to identify as "mumtrepreneurs".

She considers that when family dynamics work well this makes it easier for the family business to be successful, but when there are disagreements and friction then many problems arise that can damage the family, and other relationships as well as the business itself. She also added that another advantage of family business is the ability to share difficulties and problems for the long-term benefit of the family. Matija has never been in a family business but has seen many and feels that they should be treated case by case.

QUOTES FROM WOMEN ENTREPRENEURS

- *"People respond well to those that are sure of what they want."*, **Anna Wintour, editor-in-Chief, American Vogue**
- *"Whatever it is that you think you want to do, and whatever it is that you think stands between you and that, stop making excuses. You can do anything."*, **Katia Beauchamp, co-founder and CEO, Birchbox.**
- *"Dear optimist, pessimist, and realist: While you guys were busy arguing about the glass of wine, I drank it! Sincerely, the opportunist!"*, **Lori Greiner, inventor, QVC host and 'Shark Tank' investor.**
- *"Invite people into your life that don't look or think like you."*, **Mellody Hobson, president of Ariel Investments.**
- *"I never dreamed about success. I worked for it."*, **Estée Lauder**
- *"The difference between successful people and others is how long they spend time feeling sorry for themselves."*, **Barbara Corcoran, real estate magnate and 'Shark Tank' investor.**
- *"Life-fulfilling work is never about the money -- when you feel true passion for something, you instinctively find ways to nurture it."*, **Eileen Fisher, fashion designer.**
- *"Surround yourself with a trusted and loyal team. It makes all the difference."*, **Alison Pincus, co-founder, One Kings Lane**
- *"What I wanted was to be allowed to do the thing in the world that I did best--which I believed then and believe now is the greatest privilege there is. When I did that, success found me."*, **Debbi Fields, the creator of Mrs. Fields.**
- *"Find the smartest people you can and surround yourself with them."*, **Marissa Meyer, CEO, Yahoo!**
- *"Don't be intimidated by what you don't know. That can be your greatest strength and ensure that you do things differently from everyone else."*, **Sara Blakely, founder, Spanx**
- *"Your job as leader is to stay as close in touch as possible with those closest to the action."*, **Kat Cole, president, Focus Brands**
- *"One of the most important things I have learned is that businesses don't fail, entrepreneurs give up. Now sometimes, giving up is the right decision. But usually, you just need to dig in and figure out how to make things better. Remember: Every day is a new opportunity to get up and do it better than yesterday!"*, **Adda Birnir, founder and instructor, Skillcrush**

- *"True leadership stems from individuality that is honestly and sometimes imperfectly expressed... Leaders should strive for authenticity over perfection."*, **Sheryl Sandberg, COO, Facebook**
- *"I know society says you should be a certain way, but I think [you should] stop and look at what is your natural way of being who you are."*, **Ari Horie, founder, Women's StartUp Lab**
- *"It's up to us to all challenge our own boundaries, our own comfort zones, and get out and see what else is out there in the world and what else is possible, and give ourselves a shot to go a little bit deeper, a little bit further."*, **Jennifer Kushell, founder and CEO of Young & Successful Media and YSN.com (Your Success Now)**
- *"Our fear of the unknown and our fear of making mistakes trick us into focusing on what we don't know or can't do. When we give ourselves the freedom to be uncertain and less than perfect, then we can start thinking, 'What do I know? What can I do?' That's when the adventure starts -- learning, thriving, conquering, failing, recouping, and having a ton of fun."*, **Kristin Smith, COO, Dolly, Inc.**
- *"Treating people with kindness and respect seems elementary but is not always reciprocated. I often run into people who tell me a story about how I impacted their life -- most often by an act of kindness that they never forgot."*, **April Uchitel, chief brand officer, Spring**
- *"People don't take opportunities because the timing is bad, the financial side unsecure. Too many people are overanalysing. Sometimes you just have to go for it."*, **Michelle Zatlyn, Co-founder of Cloudflare**

Source: Inc.com (2021)

Authors' note: many of the above came out in our interviews with the 15 interviewees.

Alan Manly OAM

From an IT tech to the founder and owner of GCA / UBSS, Australia's 7th largest MBA school

INTRODUCTION

Key points from the interview

- The most valuable element of a successful business is the customer, but not all customers are worth having.
- Be aware of, and respect your staff, your customers and those who refer work to you.
- Business is business, focus on providing the service that is the core of your business. Respect can mean minding your own business.
- When considering taking legal action, do so with your eyes wide open. Two parties involved always give a 50/50 chance.

- If you run out of cash that's the end of your business. Tradition, staff satisfaction, customer satisfaction, social conscience, all amount to naught when you run out of cash.
- If your organisation comprises several divisions do a cost benefit analysis to determine whether you should continue with all, some or none.
- Management by walking around is still the way. A visit to a work place can tell you a lot.
- Just like joining a gym, being an entrepreneur will only work if you do. It's a lifestyle decision — and so is starting a business.
- You won't achieve your dream unless you plan, commit and follow through, even on days when you would rather stay in bed.

Alan Manly OAM

Alan Manly is the founder and managing director of Group Colleges of Australia (GCA), which includes the Universal Business School of Sydney (UBSS).

Further information

- *www.alanmanly.com.au*
- *www.GCA.edu.au*
- *www.UBSS.edu.au*

Category

Traditional Entrepreneur - which came about by working in the IT Industry and taking advantage of unexpected opportunities as they came along – Hence he is also known an *"Unlikely Entrepreneur"* or an *"Accidental entrepreneur"*.

The by-line of Alan's latest book *"The Unlikely Entrepreneur"* states *"How you can start with nothing, break all the rules and create a business empire"*. Like the title of his book, he indeed is an unlikely entrepreneur, but he became successful by utilising his skills, experience and taking up opportunities as they came.

Alan is a Justice of the Peace (JP) and a Fellow of the Australian Institute of Company Directors (FAICD) and has over the years been active in representing the industry and is a former Director of the Australian Council of Private Education and Training (ACPET) and a former Board member of a national Higher Education industry representative body, now called the Independent Higher Education Australia (IHEA). Alan was honoured in the Queen's Birthday 2021 Honours List with the Medal of the Order of Australia (OAM) for his contribution to tertiary education.

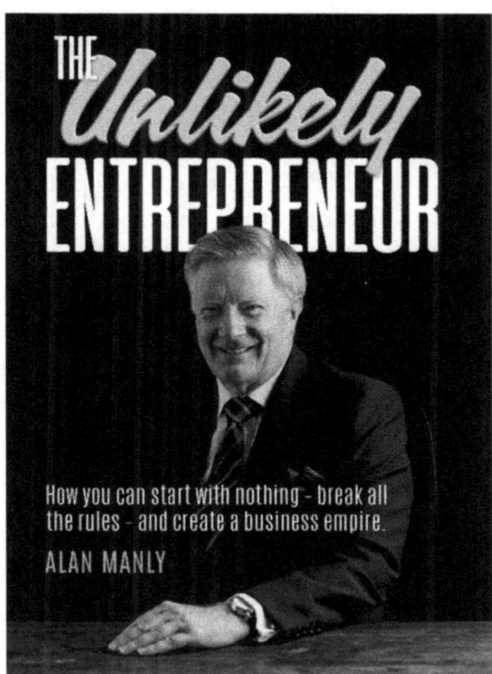

Figure 34 - Cover of the "Unlikely Entrepreneur" book

One of Alan's many published articles is referenced in the below link. It is a quick summary of some salient lessons and harsh truths about business success that everyone thinking of going into business should read:

https://www.smartcompany.com.au/business-advice/harsh-truth-entrepreneurship/

In reviewing the book Ross Cameron, the Skynews *"Outsiders"* host summarised it well when he said, *"This is business as it should be taught – in the raw. For those who want to act, not talk. Littered with gold nuggets."*

I. KEY DATES

- 1960s: Bacchus Marsh High School Melbourne Victoria
- 1971: Electronics RMIT University
- 1977: Computer Engineer Boston USA
- 1979 Promotion to Senior Executive position

- 1986: Had an "entrepreneurial seizure" and left his corporate career to join a software company addressing the transport industry.
- 1988: Educational Holdings assigned management contract for MBC School of Computer Studies to be located at 5 Belmore Street Burwood NSW 2134.
- 1989: MBC School of Computer Studies acquired by Educational Holdings. Alan Manly, Co-Director.
- 1990: Educational Holdings was renamed as NSW Business College. Alan's wife Jenny McCarthy joined the NSW Business College management team. Later she became the GCA General Manger.
- 1996: Alan Manly and Jenny McCarthy resigned as NSW Business College Directors and Alan sold his shares. The NSW Business College was renamed Australia Business Technology Institute (ABTI) by its new owners.
- 1998: Group Colleges Australia (GCA) established, with Alan as Managing Director
- 2004: GCA celebrated its five years, and Central College established as major education exporter
- 2008: GCA, trading as Universal International College (UIC) Sydney, obtained its Higher Education Providers Licence. GCA commenced delivering the Bachelor of Accounting Degree. This was accredited by IPA Australia (Institute of Public Accountants) in 2009, and CPA (Certified Practising Accountants) Australia and the Chartered Accountants Australia & New Zealand (CA ANZ) in 2010.
- 2010: GCA relocated to a new 5,000 sqm building which was the former TNT Twin Towers at one 1 Lawson Square Redfern Sydney, an inner-city suburb.

- 2011: Alan's book "When there are too many lawyers …" published. It is about a catastrophic legal disaster that very nearly bankrupted Alan. This was over a dispute relating to a $115 cheque, which resulted in 250 court appearances over a 10-year period and cost him hundreds of thousands of dollars and nearly bankrupted his family. The journey went from the Local Court in North Sydney to the High Court of Australia. Alan and his co-defendant represented themselves and won all thirty-two cases. Along the way the claimant was convicted of fraud, assault, and ending in being declared a vexatious litigant.
- 2012: Renamed Universal International College Sydney to Universal Business School Sydney (UBSS).
- 2016: Relocation of colleges to the heart of Sydney's CBD: UBSS relocated to Level 10 and 11 at 233 Castlereagh Street Sydney; Metro English College relocated to Level 4, 127 Liverpool Street Sydney; and Central College relocated to Level 5, 127 Liverpool Street Sydney
- 2018: Alan's book "The unlikely entrepreneur" published. It is about Alan's story, which basically is "from an IT technician to the founder and owner of GCA / UBSS, Australia's 7th largest MBA school".
- 2018: Group Colleges Australia (GCA) elected to change its strategic direction and decided to concentrate on higher education, being undergraduate and postgraduate courses and closed the Central College and Metro English Colleges in December of 2018.
- June 2021 the UBSS Executive Delivery MBA expanded to Melbourne and is expected to soon follow with a Brisbane initiative.
- June 2021: Honoured in the Queen's Birthday 2021 Honours List with the Medal of the Order of Australia (OAM)
- Late 2021: Group Colleges of Australia, trading as Universal Business School of Sydney, "UBSS", is the nation's 7th largest Master of Business Administration (MBA) school. With a successful expansion into Melbourne in June 2021 and potential expansion soon in Brisbane Alan confidently expects UBSS to grow over time and have a higher ranking.

II. GETTING TO KNOW THE PERSON

1. What is success?

Alan summarises success as a "well provided for family", that is providing security to his family. He explains that security is more than financial and includes psychological security. He gives the example that it may be better to live in an overcapitalised house in the area you feel comfortable in rather than a huge mansion where you "feel like a fish out of water". He also stated that the above security may vary depending on the life stage of the key family members.

Authors' note: See the Australian movie "The Castle" which explains this concept perfectly

He ended this question by saying that his company provides education in the form of an MBA for entrepreneurs, with his graduates going on to follow their dreams in business. Alan feels that with 500 graduates each year, his work is done

2. What is your favourite TV show, movie or book and why?

- Television:
    - *Yes Minister*
    - *A Touch of Frost*
    - *History Channel*
- Movie: *The Castle*
- Book: David Saul Alinsky's *Rules for Radicals: A Pragmatic Primer* (1971)

3. What are your hobbies and/or Interests?

His hobby is business. Alan is also very interested in politics. He enjoys those cleverly made television shows such as Yes Minister and the History Channel, as well as David Saul Alinsky's book that discusses issues on our big picture social structures.

III. TIPS

4. How did you get through your worst times?

The below link[7] refers to an article that discusses his worst times. "When Sydney businessman Alan Manly received an unexpected invoice for $115, he had no idea it would lead to a 10-year court battle and end up costing him hundreds of thousands of dollars. What the then not-for-profit director thought would be a simple bill dispute spiralled out of control and ended up in Australia's highest court with the epic battle costing him, his business partner Julian Day, and his family in more ways than one. Representing themselves, the pair endured 250 court appearances over 34 cases that Mr Manly estimates cost him in excess of $200,000 and millions in opportunity costs over the ten years. It was "very costly socially as well". "I was at a point in my life where I was a successful businessman in my 40s. I had a house in a middle-class suburb with a swimming pool out the back and a Mercedes Benz in the driveway, and it all fell apart. I was devastated."

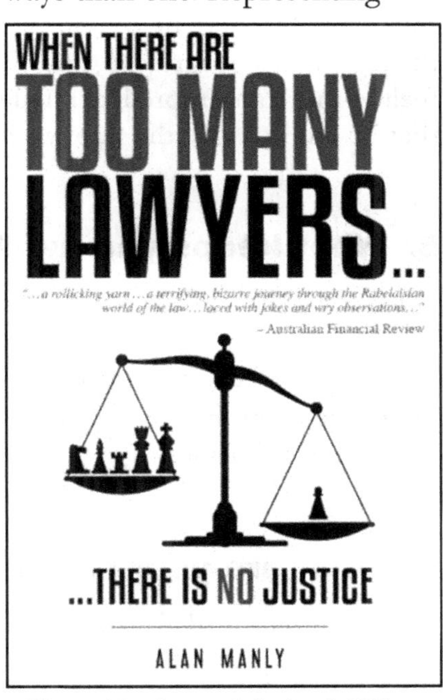

Figure 35 - Cover of the book "When there are too many lawyers"

When asked about how he got through his worst times Alan responded that "he needed therapy", and that is why he wrote the book *"When there are too many lawyers"*.

He said while writing the book was difficult, it was a liberating experience and allowed him to put the tumultuous decade behind him. He said the whole experience still haunted him. "It took 10 of

7 *https://static1.squarespace.com/static/535dd934e4b0586b1fc72324/t/543356 11e4b07597e9ebff5b/1412650513024/Alan+Manly+article+on+news.com.au+5+October+2014.pdf*, viewed 7th August 2021

the best years of our lives," and "I was on the brink of bankruptcy, it left my entire family traumatised. It was only after I read the ninth manuscript of the book that I could do so without crying." And while he certainly isn't anti-lawyer and uses them in business dealings, he has one word of advice for anyone considering taking legal action. "Do it with your eyes wide open," he said.

Knowing that this interview will be read by students considering higher studies, going into business or both, Alan elaborated saying that the "10-year court battle" was an unfortunate situation where he was trapped and felt he could only move with the tide. He said normally the hero is a person who volunteers to risk his or her life for others but here he did not volunteer but was trapped, and as the legal cases progressed, and the legal fees added up, he began feeling more and more like a failure. Alan said that he was lucky that he did not lose the family's house and all their possessions.

5. What keeps you awake at night?

Alan said that after all these years cash flow still keeps him awake. To this day his office still provides him with a daily cash flow analysis. After what he experienced with his court cases, he has an insecurity regarding cash flow. He dryly states: "If your money ends so does your business".

6. What are your typical daily routines?

Alan said that his daily office routine is:

- Check emails
- Communicate with people as to what needs to be done, starting with the most important issues
- Where necessary he will consult with one of his two key executives.

7. What advice would you give yourself starting out?

He advised:

- The most valuable element of a successful business is the customer. Run an ad for staff and many apply. Running an ad to attract customers is always a much bigger challenge, observing that staff are much easier to obtain than customers.
- Not all customers are worth having. If they are not prepared to pay in full, or pay on time for your goods and services, they may be costing more than they are worth and thus you may want to get rid of them.
- Focus on cash flow, cash flow, cash flow, and then cash flow, as with a strong cash flow you can keep trading. A business collapses when it run out of cash. Tradition, staff satisfaction, customer satisfaction, social conscience, all amount to naught when you run out of cash.
- The CEO's office is potentially the happiest room in the building, and this is not necessarily a good thing because there are many people bringing only good news. It is important to focus on the goals of that department to avoid being distracted and drowned in only good news.
- "If you don't go, you won't know". Management by walking around is still the way. A visit to a workplace can tell you a lot. He especially looks for the "vibe" as he feels that it can tell you so much about the organisation.
- Look, and take, opportunities. He has done this over and over in his career.

IV. BUSINESS CASE EXAMPLES

8. Provide a case you managed well and why?

As we saw in the chronology at the beginning of this interview, in 2010 GCA moved into the 5000 square meter Redfern buildings campus. Because it had 5000 students it was a very busy place, as the campus had a high school, an English college, a vocational education college and higher education school. This created problems including noise, where noisy high school kids were not compatible with MBA students. Alan considered the matter and closed the high school down. The organisation's headquarters left Redfern in 2016 and went to its current premises, at 233 Castlereagh Street, Sydney. The organisation was reduced to three campuses:

- The Metro English College at Level 4, 127 Liverpool Street Sydney
- The vocational education Central College at Level 5, 127 Liverpool Street Sydney
- Higher education at 233 Castlereagh Street Sydney,

The three new individual campuses allowed exacting cost analysis. Alan made a simple cost benefit analysis of each of the campuses. From this analysis it became quite clear that a focus on the higher education component was sensible as it was relatively easy to run, it was profitable and had a good future. From this analysis it became a simple process of keeping the higher education campus and closing the other two campuses. As all three were owned by the same entity it would have been too difficult legally to sell the two unwanted businesses and in December 2018 they were simply closed down. Having closed the two businesses down meant that three quarters of the organisation's staff were retrenched. Alan organised that a very senior executive in the company of external experts spoke to each staff member in order to explain the situation stating it wasn't personal but business and assisted staff in their transition out of the organisation.

9. Provide a case that did not go well and why?

The organisation recently set up a satellite campus in Thailand to test the market for online learning. However, online learning was traditionally not permitted in Thailand causing some difficulties, with client acceptance. COVID fortunately changed the reality such that online learning is now allowed and had to be accepted. The whole project was expensive and time consuming. One benefit from this venture is that this enhanced the research and development for the running of other satellite campuses and online courses without damaging the core business.

10. What conclusions can be drawn by comparing these cases?

- In the case of the Sydney campuses, the locations developed organically and with a systematic approach.
- By contrast the Thailand experiment was a little rushed and it would have been easier, less expensive and better to set up an online satellite Melbourne campus, than to go overseas to set this up. But the risk would have been learning in your home market.

11. What cultural issues did you experience? How were they overcome? How is Australia different? Were these cases affected by.

Alan considers that within UBSS the organisation experienced a number of cultural issues including:

- *Students*: the organisation has students to from 30 different countries and the number of students and countries of origin is growing due to its focus on the "customers", that is the students. Alan says he expects his staff to be professional in their appearance as in dress professionally, and behaviour and expects high quality teaching from staff. Specifically, he advises staff that the following are compulsory (noting that what he expects often does not occur in Australian universities): his staff must wear a suit and tie (or female equivalent); staff cannot be absent from classes except for exceptional reasons; students are to be treated like customers; and what is taught today needs to be able to be used at work tomorrow.
- *Staff*: Alan stated that many staff are from overseas. He said that staff are treated well, and there are many cultural differences in the organisation. An Asian staff member was asked about working at the organisation. She responded stating that she liked many things including that the CEO, Alan, says hello noting that in Asia this does not often occur, and feels that this is proof of mutual respect. Other positive things are that the organisation is very structured and is essentially a family business.

- *Students and Staff*: When one walks through the office one sees the Australian flag. Alan stressed that this is because the business is about international education but with a focus on Australia. Alan notes that students and staff are very keen on this international flavour, and inclusive way the business is run. He points to the low staff turnover rate as an indicator that staff are happy.
- *Overseas Agents:* (They co-ordinate and recommend the UBSS courses to overseas students: In addition to staff and students, which were discussed above, he states the other key group is agents. The organisation invests significant time to educate, develop and build links with good Agents. They are vitally important to the success of the GCA / UBSS.
- *Online learning:* The organisation's online learning has been very successful. The Deloittes university survey showed 70% student satisfaction, but with Alan's organisation it has been an outstanding 90% satisfaction.

V. VOLATILITY (FOR EXAMPLE COVID)

12. How has the virus affected your business?

Unfortunately, the COVID-19 pandemic has hit the business hard. In August 2021 its revenues were down 60% from pre-pandemic times. However, from the outset the organisation was mindful of managing risk and did several sensible things. The first is that it sought students from a diverse range of countries, and this was very helpful when China sought to dissuade students from studying in Australia. The second was sourcing local and overseas students living locally (referred to as onshore students). This latter strategy helped to mitigate against the loss of students due to COVID prevention measures which closed international borders. Some of the Australian universities have had major problems due to students being unable to attend Australian universities, and thus had to let substantial numbers of staff go. It is to the credit of the organisation that not one staff member has been let go during the current pandemic.

13. What lasting impact do you think it will have on your business?

The impact has been significant. Australian international education is a $40 billion export business which quickly halved. Fortunately, classes can still be taught online but the revenue to the various education providers, and indeed the country, is substantially less than it was prior to the pandemic.

14. What have you learned from it that you will now implement in your business?

The organisation has learnt the importance of being flexible in managing the online and blended learning settings and being able to quickly adapt to changes going on around them.

VI. FAMILY BUSINESS

15. Are you in a family business and from your experience what do you think are the advantages and disadvantages of family working in the business?

Alan does not really see the organisation (that is, GCA / UBSS) currently as being a family business. Alan's wife, Jennifer was working in the business and took a very active role in the business helping to get the higher education licence. She has since retired. Alan's son, James only works part time at UBSS.

Alan is positive about the strengths and culture of a family business and thinks it is a powerful way to run a business as long as the appropriate advice and expertise is properly considered. It may of course be a benevolent dictatorship. Interestingly this is not unwelcomed to a customer base for Asia.

Authors' note: Alan's attitude about the strengths is not dissimilar to that of many other interviewees.

Figure 36 - Alan, Jennifer and James Manly

FUN FACTS ON: NOT QUITE RIGHT

Did not get it right: The telephone

- *"What use would this company make of an electrical toy?"*, **Carl Orton, President of Western Union**, to Alexander Graham Bell, who offered all rights to the telephone for $100,000
- *"This telephone has too many shortcomings to be seriously considered as a means of communication"*, Western Union internal memo. 1876

Did get it right: Microwave cooking

- Article from Popular Mechanics: Prediction 1937: Microwave Cooking, *"Cooking a ham sandwich in high-frequency radio waves. This method may be common in the home of the future."*

Source: Popular Mechanics (2021)

Jon Tse

From renting textbooks to transforming recycled stone into paper

INTRODUCTION

Key points from the interview

- "If you are going through hell, keep going" (Winston Churchill) – why bother stopping in a bad place? Keep charging through until you are in a good spot.
- "When things are going well in business, always keep in mind there are probably some storm clouds brewing. But also keep in mind that sunshine follows the rain, so it is important to always be optimistically realistic" (Jon Tse)
- When asking others for advice, choose to ask those that have walked down the path that you wish to take, as they will have a more relevant set of experiences and mindsets.
- Launching a business is like pushing a rock up the hill. It is never easy work, but you can make it easier by making the hill less and less of an incline. People, systems and of course sales growth helps this.

- In business think where the "ball" should be rather than where it is now.
- Be prepared to make mistakes but do your best to make the best decision given the information you have. It is near impossible to execute flawlessly throughout the life of the business.
- Without mistakes there is no progress so you cannot be frozen in fear about making a mistake because there will be no progress at all!

Jon Tse

Jon studied a Bachelor of Professional Accounting and Bachelor of Laws at Macquarie University in Sydney, Australia under a Mitsui Education Foundation scholarship. He started interning at a big four accounting firm, followed by completing his CPA at a big four bank, however it did not take long for the entrepreneur in him to escape. He started up a student resume business whilst working full-time in the corporate world, which quickly overtook his banking salary and led to launching an education technology company which grew to revenues over $30M and over 40 staff. More recently, Jon has launched an Australian consumer brand called Karst, which transforms recycled stone into beautiful stationery products for the home and workplace.

Further information

- *https://www.karststonepaper.com*
- *https://www.news.com.au/finance/business/retail/karst-a-million-dollar-business-that-emerged-from-a-holiday-discovery/news-story/a73651732bbeba000ef14a516b58ab0b*

Category

Innovative entrepreneurship. Innovative entrepreneurs are people who are constantly coming up with new ideas and inventions. They take these ideas and turn them into business ventures. They often aim to change the way people live for the better. Innovators tend to be very motivated and passionate people. They look for ways to make their products and services stand out from other things on the market. People like Steve Jobs and Bill Gates are examples of innovative entrepreneurs. *https://www.indeed.com/career-advice/career-development/types-of-entrepreneurship*

I. KEY DATES

- 1987: Born in Sydney, Australia
- 2006: Entered Macquarie University as an undergraduate
- 2008: Became President of the Asia-Pacific Entrepreneurship Society and attended student summits at Stanford University & Peking University
- 2009: Obtained Mitsui Education Scholarship and interned at KPMG in Corporate Tax
- 2011: Completed a Bachelor of Professional Accounting with Bachelor of Laws and started as a graduate at NAB in Sydney.
- 2012: Whilst at NAB, completed his CPA.
- 2013: Launched a side hustle business helping university students with their cover letters and resumes until this business overtook my banking salary and decided to go full-time into entrepreneurship.
- 2013: Co-founded textbook rental business (Zookal) with two friends from university
- 2015: Zookal team grew to 25 staff, acquiring a competitor business
- 2016: Moved to Singapore to expand Zookal into South East Asia growing out digital tools and resources
- 2017: Whilst living in Singapore, was visited by a school friend who showed me this new, sustainable and alternative material (stone paper)
- 2018: Visited Taiwan to see the creator of stone paper in a regional city called Tainan and became an advisor to the newly launched brand, Karst.
- 2019: Returned to Sydney and joined Karst full-time as a co-founder after falling in love with the mission and brand.

- 2020: Raised funding for Karst from the founders of Canva and Envato (Australian tech unicorns) and launched Karst warehouses in Sydney, Netherlands and Amsterdam
- 2021: Reached first 50,000 Karst customers in over 90 countries and hired ex-Moleskine sales executive in Karst London office
- 2021: Secured distribution deals in Australia & the UK and to be launched in Staples US & Canada
- 2021: the company's website provides details of the product (see photograph, below), which can be summarised as:
    - *Better when wetter*: Karst Stone Paper™ is completely waterproof. So, your morning coffee can't ruin your eureka moment, and the rain can't steal your thunder.
    - *Not just recycled. Up-cycled*: Our paper is made from calcium carbonate, a repurposed construction waste. Our process has been redesigned to eliminate elements of waste that would have been unavoidable in the traditional paper-making process.
    - *Smoother doesn't begin to describe it*: Our paper is friction-free, pens glide across our pages because there is no grain direction.
    - *Smaller footprint made smaller again*: Our paper has a 67% smaller carbon footprint.
    - *We keep our colour all natural*: Our paper is naturally bright white, never dyed or bleached with harsh chemicals like chlorine or acid.

Figure 37 - www.karststonepaper.com

II. GETTING TO KNOW THE PERSON

1. What is success?

Jon finds it hard to define what success is. He thinks that the goal posts are moving. When he was younger it was making a sale. Now it is making many big sales. He feels that success is not an end point, but a mind set (called a "vanity metric"), which is something in your head which you change to reality so others can see. Interestingly he speaks about success in relation to getting advice. He stated that when he thought about going into business family and friends were invariably negative coming up with many reasons why he should not to go ahead. He said that generally these people had a conservative mindset, which is different from an entrepreneur, who needs a risk mind set to succeed. He felt it was better to consult with people who have already walked down the path that he wishes to take.

Authors' note: it is very sensible to ask a number of people who have walked down the path that you wish to take. Ask where they went well and where they could have done better. Get as much information from as many people as you can before starting.

2. What is your favourite TV show, movie or book and why?

- Books:
  - Hard copy: *Shantaram* (a 2003 autobiographical novel by Gregory Roberts about live on the run in India):
  - Audio books:
    - *Green Lights* – Matthew McConaughey's audio book
    - *Shoe Dog* – about Phil Knight, the co-founder of Nike
    - *Ride of a Lifetime* - Robert Iger, the former CEO of Disney.
- TV: Does not watch much, but when he does, he likes to watch Scandinavian detective shows, such as *The Bridge*

- Favourite movie: *Hurricane*, a sport and crime movie set in the 1960s - 1980s.
- Podcast: Jon was inspired by Guy Raz's podcast on starting a business *"How I built this resilience series"*: *https://www.youtube.com/watch?v=wd0kweDLJyE*

3. What are your hobbies and/or Interests?

Jon is an active person, he played soccer until he was 25. He's often outdoors jogging or going to the gym. He loves to see progression whether it is in business, or in his personal life.

III. TIPS

4. How did you get through your worst times?

He feels that he is blessed because he is resilient, optimistic and works very hard. He feels he's been to hell and back in business especially in his mid-20s. He refers to Winston Churchill statement's "If you are going to go through hell, keep going". Jon says that when things are going well, he's got to watch out because there are probably storm clouds on the way.

5. What keeps you awake at night?

Nothing much keeps Jon awake at night. He's trained himself to switch off. He's aware that he's running a marathon and not a sprint. If something does worry him during the night, he writes it down and returns to it in the morning as he tries not to fret about things at night, because he knows not much can be done about them.

6. What are your typical daily routines?

He's normally up at 7 am and at work 8 and works until 6 pm. He knows that he is an entrepreneur, and tries not to work 24/7 as that is not good for him nor the business. However, if he has to do so, then he will do it. He feels the day does not have to be rigidly set but he feels it's a successful day if he's had a solid day at work and does some physical activity. He realises that flexibility is important, but an unfortunate part of his work is after-hours international calls. This includes the need to communicate with investors, suppliers and customers. He has offices in the USA and UK. He is now working on delegating certain functions to team members.

7. What advice would you give yourself starting out?

Almost without hesitation he said that be prepared to make every mistake in the book, but you may not realise that you've made a mistake. He said that in starting a business you need to realise that technology rules the world but, he prefers physical products. He said that launching a business is like pushing a rock up the hill. He said it's never easy work, but you can make it easier by making the hill less inclined. He refers to the ice hockey coach's advice that "the player needs to think where the puck should be rather than where it is now". He advocates knowing how to leverage technology and be a disruptor, that is how to get your foot in the market door and work hard ensuring that you make the hill a little less steep.

Figure 38 - Kevin Garcia and Jon Tse, Karst® co-founders

Our design process starts with a simple question. Why?

Why does paper need to be made out of trees? Why can't journals be waterproof? Why are we still using paper-making practices that were cutting edge in the 16th century?

Why can't we do better?

https://www.karststonepaper.com/

IV. BUSINESS CASE EXAMPLES

8. Provide a case you managed well and why?

As we all know unfortunate events occur. Jon states that one needs to be vigilant and take risks when necessary to exploit opportunities. He gave the following hand sanitiser case as an example of where things went well. He said that when the pandemic started there was a huge increase in demand for hand sanitiser, with frequent shortages. Through a contact he was able to buy bulk sanitiser, and then had it converted into 20,000 bottles with 18,000 sold and 2,000 given to charity.
https://www.businessinsider.com.au/karst-stationery-hand-sanitizer-shortages-australia-2020-4?r=US&IR=T

9. Provide a case that did not go well and why?

Jon states that when they were growing fast in the early days of Zookal, he looked to hire quickly to help foster this growth and take advantage of the unique opportunity the business presented. However, he learned the hard way the saying "hire slow and fire quickly". He stresses that Rome was not built in a day and to build the right foundations it is imperative to get the right people on the train and not just 'anyone' will do, as it will eventually come back to bite you. The business has different personnel requirements at different stages. Some people are suited for early days of a fast-growing business, some people and their skills are better suited for later-stage companies, but it is really up to the founders and management teams to find the right people at the right time of the business.

10. What conclusions can be drawn by comparing these cases?

He feels that hindsight is a wonderful thing, so expect problems and eat them for breakfast! Be prepared to make mistakes but do your best to make the best decision given the information you have. Hopefully, the mistakes you make can be lessons learned and don't prove to be too costly for the business in the long run. Having said that, without mistakes there is no progress so you cannot be frozen in fear about making a mistake because there will be no progress at all!

Authors' note: An important point for all aspiring entrepreneurs!

11. What cultural issues did you experience? How were they overcome? How is Australia different? Were these cases affected by.

Jon was born and raised in Sydney from an Asian family. Jon said they made a mistake when pitching for funds by using the methods that they had used in Australia, that is they were too humble and down to earth. He said the Americans love to add bravado and hyperbole as to why the investors should put money into the business. They were there for two and a half weeks and had between 30 and 40 meetings, and notwithstanding their lack of histrionics they were successful in that one investor invested 1.5 million US Dollars. Jon pointed out when he went back to his family and told them they asked him whether he was a snake oil salesman. Jon was worried that his father would not approve, and he kept on dressing for work pretending to go to his bank job every day but he in fact was going to his co-founded business. This continued until he took his father to the new business.

V. VOLATILITY (FOR EXAMPLE COVID)

12. How has the virus affected your business?

In speaking about volatility Jon spoke about the COVID pandemic. The pandemic occurred about the time they raised money from the Canva & Envato founders and Karst just launched a new website to go into retail. He stated that their product, stone paper books, is a tactile product and it is best sold retail, that is through department stores galleries, museums, train stations etc. He found that COVID put a hold on this. Another unfortunate situation was that they were working through a distribution agreement at that time relating to access to about 2000 stores around Australia and New Zealand. This is on hold until the shops reopen. Jon said this is a big wake up call. He said that sh*t happens and if it does then one needs to be prepared to go with your gut feel and move quickly and take risks. He gave the example of the demand for hand sanitiser when the pandemic started, and this was discussed in question 8, above.

13. What lasting impact do you think it will have on your business?

Due to the necessity of inventory being in physical stores, or sold through trade shows, where the physical item can be inspected the volatility of the COVID pandemic will have a lasting effect on business. Prior to the pandemic there was a 100% year on year increase. The pandemic is not the only volatility. Another potential issue is the tension between USA, China and Taiwan. Jon's organisation has agreements with Taiwan who helped to pioneer the technology and helped to develop the market. At this stage there does not appear to much of a Chinese impact on their business. Tariffs have increased from 10% to 25% on their product from Taiwan to USA. Jon states that as their products are premium products (they seek the best quality) price is not such an issue, but quality is. They have spread their logistics risks by having warehouses in Australia, USA and Amsterdam.

14. What have you learned from it that you will now implement in your business?

Jon says that the COVID pandemic has taught us that there are no rules in business and that anything can happen. He said that luckily, they have three ways to sell. The first is retail sales direct to the customer, the second is wholesale to book shops stationary stores etc, and the third is business to business which is customised logos and corporate gifting. This was not planned, but it turned out beneficial for the company. The combined effect of these three ways to sell means that the company has made enough sales to keep staff busy, so therefore no staff have been laid off due to the COVID-19 pandemic. If one distribution channel slows there is another one that can compensate. This helps to recue volatility in the business. He said that in business you need to be quick because sometimes growth areas appear, and you need to take advantage of them when you can.

Authors' note: You recall that Warrier, our first interviewee, who owns two Sydney Harbour showboats had no income for a number of months. Jon's business was fortunate because, unlike with Warrier's business, it had three different ways of marketing their goods and thus was able to keep the business going, make profits and not have to put staff off.

Jon says that despite Covid and market volatility, there are still lots of opportunities, but you just need to be nimble enough to take advantage.

Authors' further note: We once had a client that loved chaos because the client felt they had the ability to find the gaps and opportunities better than others.

VI. FAMILY BUSINESS

15. Are you in a family business and from your experience what do you think are the advantages and disadvantages of family working in the business?

Jon advised that he's not in a family business. He's not keen on family working in a business because there are two contradictory relationships, the family and the business. He prefers there not to be a family relationship. He elaborates stating the disadvantage of a family business is that if something goes wrong with the business it affects the family. This is a risk he's not keen on taking.

He notes that he has observed well-functioning family businesses, particularly large ones. Jon says big businesses and small start-ups have a different dynamic which may affect how easy it is for family members to fit in.

Figure 39 - image from www.karststonepaper.com website

Comment from the website:

Whether Elon likes it or not, we're all going to have to live on this planet for a while yet. To us, that means living with it, too. Putting back some of what we've all taken. So, in addition to the environmental benefits of stone paper, Karst is B Corp Certified, has partnered with the One Tree Planted Foundation and is 100% Carbon Neutral

FUN FACTS ON: CALCIUM CARBONATE

(Note that Karst Stone Paper™ is made from calcium carbonate)

- *Calcium carbonate is one of the most common minerals.* Calcium carbonate makes up 4% of the earth's crust. Over 20% of the World's sedimentary rocks are composed of chalk or limestone.
- *Calcium carbonate – plant or animal or both?* Limestone is an inorganic, sedimentary rock formed from the remains of microscopic animals or foraminifera. Chalk was also thought to be derived from foraminifera but in 1953 was shown to be largely composed of coccoliths, a lime-secreting algae. So, both.
- *The world's oldest building is made of calcium carbonate.* Khufu's Pyramid, usually referred to as the "Great Pyramid", is the world's oldest structure and consists of 2.5 million limestone blocks, each one weighing an average of 2.5 tonnes.
- *Chalk whiting – a Saxon connection.* Ground Chalk has been commonly known for centuries as Whiting. It is believed 'whiting' is derived from the Saxon word, 'Hwíting-melu', which literally means 'whitening powder'.
- *Calcium is the fifth most abundant element in the body.* Calcium is an important structural component of bones and teeth and also is necessary for the normal function of all muscles and nerves.
- *When pasta was made from chalk.* Pasta, the Italian term for dough, originally referred to how painters produced their pastel chalk. They kneaded chalk, pigment powder and an aqueous binder into uniform dough from which pencils were formed and finally dried.
- *Calcium carbonate exists only on Earth and possibly on Mars.* In Shergotty, India a meteorite fell from the sky which is believed to have originated from Mars. The meteorite contained calcium carbonate, as well as traces of gypsum.
- *Blackboard chalk isn't chalk.* The base of pastel chalks is not calcium carbonate but calcium sulphate (CaSO4), which is

derived from gypsum (CaSO4-2H2O). Pastels also contain clays and oils for binding and strong pigments.

- *Chalk and Cheese – a scam in the Middle Ages.* 14th century Welsh market traders used to try to pass chalk off as a hard cheese on unsuspecting customers, hence the popular term 'like chalk & cheese'
- *The white cliffs of Dover are "rare".* Though white cliffs are fairly common in England the only other chalk cliffs in the world, are in Northern Ireland, France, Denmark and Germany. Chalk geology is rare in the World, confined to northwest Europe; thus it is of global importance.

Source: Calcium Carbonate Org (2021)

Annemarie Manders

From nursing to lavender farming

INTRODUCTION

Key points from the interview

- Start small and learn from your mistakes along the way and then expand.
- Do not get demoralised if the venture does not work, as it may not be the person. It may simply be the product is not quite right for the market
- Get up early as that can be a very productive time of the morning, and much can get done.
- Ensure you have current computer skills as technology continues to drive the world.
- Take early action if staff are not suited to the position.
- Continually evaluate all parts of the business which is good business management in any case.
- The importance of engaging a good Accountant

Annemarie Manders

Annemarie has a background in Nursing. When her family settled in Wandin, an outer suburb of Melbourne in Victoria, she had the idea of growing lavender to utilise the property, a former orchard. She had no agricultural knowledge, but a passion for being creative, productive and utilising unused land. She was keen to start immediately, take the challenge and have a hobby. With no research, she jumped in the deep end!

She had an immediate affinity to lavender with the colour, and the steady tidy growth patterns. It reminded her of her very ordered nursing in medical operating theatres.

Annemarie started with a crop of 500 plants. Her nursing income and husband, Peter's wages were used to help pay to set up and run the business. As time passed it became clear that it was not producing enough to pay its way. Annemarie then expanded the business (against some advice and opposition from family members). This proved to be the right decision and after hiring an accountant to advise on administration, she never looked back

This business continued to expand as products were added including tourism, giving people a lavender experience and presentation at shows. Annemarie is a self-admitted workaholic and loves being busy. She does not believe in copying others but rather believes in your own unique take on things. It is interesting that Annmarie purposely did not want to visit other Lavender farms and wanted to do it her own way and stresses the importance of creativity and imagination.

Further information

- *www.warratinalavender.com.au*

Category

Agritourism Entrepreneur. According to the National Ag Law Centre (2021) agritourism is a commercial enterprise that links agricultural production and/or processing with tourism in order to attract visitors onto a farm or other agricultural business for the purposes of entertaining and/or educating the visitors and generating income.

I. KEY DATES

- 1946: Annemarie was born in Melbourne immediately after WW2. As a young child she always relished the idea of being a nurse. Although her mother tried to encourage her to widen her career focus, Annemarie could not be dissuaded and consequently after completing her Matriculation (Year 12) she took up nursing.
- 1965: She enrolled at the Alfred Hospital. Annemarie's career led her to her main love, the Operating theatre specialising in all kinds of surgery.
- 1969-1974: Annemarie travelled widely, hitch-hiking throughout Europe and the UK, working as a theatre nurse in London, Germany and Switzerland. She became fluent in German. She always liked a challenge and was determined to make a success of whatever the challenge was to be.
- 1974: Annemarie briefly returned to Australia and met a man who introduced her to flying in small planes. The next challenge was to become a pilot.
- 1978: Her life changed when she married the pilot, Peter Manders. They renovated an old house on a property in Wandin, which included an old orchard, where they brought up their 2 sons.
- 1979-1995: Annemarie continued to work part time as a theatre nurse in various local hospitals.
- 1989: The idea of growing lavender came to Annemarie to utilise the old orchard. She wanted to see the land being used productively. She had no agricultural knowledge, but a passion for being creative, productive and utilising unused land. She was keen to start immediately, take the challenge and have a hobby. With no research, jumped in the deep end!
- 1994: She had planted out over 10,000 lavender plants and was developing products to sell at markets. This was a steep learning curve, ingredients, labelling, packaging, legal

requirements and costings. Also, how to do displays, and talk to people about the benefits of lavender.

- 1994-2014: Annemarie would travel to markets every weekend for nearly 20 years, getting her product out there and spreading the word about the farm.
- 1996: She built a shop on the farm as a small retail outlet.
- 1997: Her first Lavender Festival. She had no running water, no car parking and not much know-how. Despite all of this it was a huge success and subsequent festivals have continued ever since.
- 2000-2019: Annemarie has been presented with many awards in tourism and retail from The International Flower and Garden Show, Mind Body Spirit Festival, The Australian Lavender Growers Association, Regional Tourism Association, certificates of appreciation from Schools and TAFE Colleges.
- 2002: A café was added to the shop expanding the business from a hobby growing lavender to retail products to hospitality. Tourism and International visitors started. When Annemarie started the business, she never thought about going into tourism!
- 2002-2021: Big Shows were the next challenge. These included the International Flower and Garden Show, the Mind Body Spirit Festivals in all States of Australia, Garden Shows, and Agricultural Field Days. These shows have given her huge opportunities to increase her knowledge in display, presentation, marketing etc. In addition, she had entrepreneurial ideas: events on her property during the low season, including exhibitions in the drying shed ranging from patchwork quilt and craft expos, wood working wonders, photography exhibitions and art shows.
- 2019: Annemarie was asked to be part of an education program at Swinburne TAFE (Australia's Technical And Further Education which provides a wide range of predominantly vocational courses) giving lectures to students looking for career ideas and areas to be conscious of when dealing with a multi-cultural society. She ran a thriving business employing staff, and being in demand as a speaker to herb societies, garden clubs, retirement villages and clubs.

- 2020: Annemarie was a key participant in the Farms2Schools program and gave a Power Point Presentation to a number of Primary Schools during the 6-month lock-down. The concept was to introduce children to life on a farm from cattle farming, flower growing, bee keeping, cropping etc.
- 2021: Having leased the Tea Room, Annemarie spends more time on the farm and concentrating on the retail side of the business. COVID has reduced the number of visitors but has allowed her to focus on promoting the online shop, developing the product image and initiating new on-farm event ideas.

Figure 40 - Fresh bunches of lavender hanging ready to dry

Note that she grows two different varieties of lavender which flower one month apart. The first is at the end of November where most is harvested over 10 days, and the second variety is at the end of December where the harvest again is over 10 days with a small quantity unharvested for visitors to see how they grow. The Lavender farm is about giving visitors, particularly city visitors, an experience in all the benefits of lavender cultivation.

II. GETTING TO KNOW THE PERSON

1. What is success?

Annemarie sees success as creating something, promoting it and having it accepted in the market. She feels that to go from imagining to having the business name well recognised is a great buzz.

Authors' note: as opposed to the bees buzzing on the Lavender farm.

Also, she gets this buzz from just having the energy to put into a venture, and the belief and passion is success in itself, that is, "the journey".

2. What is your favourite TV show, movie or book and why?

- Television: Annemarie does not watch much TV, maybe the occasional Quiz shows and general knowledge. She loves to learn about history, and understanding about life in earlier times.
- Movies: She is very keen on the *Sound of Music*, as it takes her back to Austria. She loves the music and particularly the song *"Climb Ev'ry Mountain"*.
- Books: She likes reading non-fiction books, including the dictionary, where she can widen her knowledge of the English language and its derivations.

3. What are your hobbies and/or Interests?

Annemarie likes gardening, embroidery, bike riding, walking. She is fond of classical music, opera, travel especially to Europe and the German language. Annemarie is active in the local Toastmasters Club, and part of the local community through CWA (Country Women's Association of Australia, which seeks the conditions for country women and children, Rotary (which seeks to bring together business and professional leaders in order to provide humanitarian service) and CFA (Country Fire Authority, which seeks to reduce the occurrence and impacts of fire and emergency services especially on the roads).

III. TIPS

4. How did you get through your worst times?

Annemarie generally tries not to let the problem get her down and focuses determining to succeed. She feels that there is always a solution. She advocates a few simple things: take the time to work out a better and more efficient way to resolve the problem. She stresses: "If you have a will, there is a way". She also advocates that you should believe in yourself and your passion and talk to others for advice. Furthermore, Annemarie says do not get demoralised if the venture does not work, as it may not be the person but simply that the product is not quite right for the market.

Authors' note: Often these things are about timing, that is, things may not work if you have the right product at the wrong time.

5. What keeps you awake at night?

Annemarie quickly responded saying "Not much." She states that she pushes herself hard during the day and by the end is physically tired and therefore falls asleep quickly. She is also a proponent of yoga relaxation exercises to assist in preparation for sleep.

6. What are your typical daily routines?

Annemarie rises before sunrise, which mostly is between 5 and 6 am, exercises, breakfasts and at the end of the day is in bed by 9.30 pm. She is a big advocate of getting up early as this for her is a very productive time, and much can be achieved because of one's freshness and lack of interruptions. Her other routines include checking emails and making lists of jobs to be done. Annemarie makes sure the house is clean and tidy before she starts the day.

She loves working and does not like to waste time. During the day she works through her to-do list.

7. What advice would you give yourself starting out?

She advises two key things.

- The first is that one should keep current with computers skills and software as technology continues to drive the world. Had such technology been available when she started, she would have researched into soil health, and weed control. We will revisit this lack of research issue in the first Case in Question 9.
- The second is that she should have allocated herself time outside of work.

IV. BUSINESS CASE EXAMPLES

8. Provide a case you managed well and why?

Annemarie has been exhibiting at various shows for some time, for example at the International Flower and Garden Show, Mind Body Spirit Festival and The Australian Lavender Growers. She advises that many of these shows happen at the same time and the first few times this occurred were very challenging for her. This is because she had to duplicate all props, shelving, tables, signage and product stock. Furthermore, she had to staff both shows with competent staff and also manage staff back at the farm/café/shop. She stated that there are many small, but vital, things that need attention including a working EFTPOS (electronic funds transfer at point of sale) machine and having a cash float (the amount of cash put in the cash drawer at the beginning of each day). To reduce the risk, she recognises that she needs to be very organised and has developed checklists and starts preparing weeks in advance and maintains a steady pace. Notwithstanding the above preparation she finds that something always goes wrong, but fortunately due to her solid preparation they are normally minor in nature. She has been successful in simultaneously conducting multiple shows, and these shows are now a major part of the business.

Figure 41 - Sydney "Mind body Spirit" festival

9. Provide a case that did not go well and why?

Case 1 – Weed control

In the early days Annemarie began the planting of lavender plants immediately after preparing the earth. Not having studied agriculture, nor easy access to computer- based knowledge, meant that the preparation was not ideal. For example, a soil analysis of trace elements and a soil pH level (an indication of the acidity or alkalinity of soil) had not been done to determine any deficiencies if any. Due to her haste in wanting to get started with growing the lavender she did not prepare the soil with a pre-emergence spray to hinder the germination of unwanted weeds and was faced with an enormous weed problem resulting in weeks and months of continual work to supress the weed problem. She stated that this is a constant battle, but it is part of farming and after 30 years she now has the hang of it! Lesson learned: take time to do your homework and not be too hasty.

Case 2 – Staffing

Selecting the right staff is never easy. Despite thorough pre-checking it is hard to know whether a staff member will work out until they are actually working. In recent times there have been a few staff issues including one after the COVID lockdown forcing some difficult decisions to be made.

Figure 42 - Pickers

10. What conclusions can be drawn by comparing these cases?

The comparison between Question 8 and Case 1 in Question 9 is clearly one of preparation in advance. She stresses that one should be organised, do your research and be careful not to be too hasty. Case 2 shows the importance of taking early action if staff are not suited to the position.

11. What cultural issues did you experience? How were they overcome? How is Australia different? Were these cases affected by.

Hospitality and Tourism at the Lavender farm has attracted many different cultures. She loves greeting people from all over the world. She says that she has had to train staff to understand what behaviour is acceptable, how to greet visitors who come from all over the world. This involves understanding dress code, food habits, toilet use. There have been issues particularly with toilet use. To overcome this during very busy times Annemarie introduced portable toilets for the coaches bringing tourists from Asia who have different toilet habits from what is the norm in Australia. The main café toilets are only accessible for café patrons by key use.

Figure 43 - Sri Lanka tourists

V. VOLATILITY (FOR EXAMPLE COVID)

12. How has the virus affected your business?

Annmarie said that COVID-19 has been a disaster as lockdowns have prevented customers visiting and therefore there have been zero international tourists. Consequently, there has been a massive reduction in income. Planning for events on the farm, permits etc then cancellations, has been costly in terms of time and money.

As a result, she has been looking at alternatives to generate income, for example more online presence with her high-profile products. Online sales have increased but fluctuate due to people's financial positions. She is trying to be more innovative and think up new ways of selling her products. She is offering more discounts to help stimulate sales. She noted that during this difficult period many people are not spending and saving their money. The government JobKeeper program has been good but not enough to stop the need to cut costs. For example, she has rented the Tea Rooms out, but due to the current situation it is closed and thus bringing in no income for the tenant. Annmarie is not charging the tenant rent during lock-down.

13. What lasting impact do you think it will have on your business?

Annemarie says she is hoping it will not have a lasting impact. There is a demand for people wanting to visit the farm and gardens, café, and planned events. She has observed people are craving to get out and have fun. In the meantime, lavender sales are on-going with wholesale and retail customers in a reduced manner. She recognises opportunities to hold functions and utilise the open space on the farm outside of the lavender flowering season. For example, Annemarie is planning a dog event with some associates, and exhibitions in the drying shed prior to the main event of the year, the Lavender Festival. These events are all promoted on the business's web site: *https://warratinalavender.com.au/events/*

14. What have you learned from it that you will now implement in your business?

Annemarie says she has learnt a lot from COVID-19 in that we need to be careful and adaptable. She is cautious with her spending and tries to save as much money as possible, stating that she has always been frugal. She believes that social distancing, wearing of masks and hand sanitation will likely be a part of our lives for some time, and advises that she has kept up to date with health regulations and any available business support packages. She furthermore advises that she has learnt the need to continually evaluate all parts of the business.

Authors' note: the need to continually evaluate all parts of the business is good business management practice and all businesses need to do it periodically in relation to the total business, and also in relation to key severable business parts.

VI. FAMILY BUSINESS

15. Are you in a family business and from your experience what do you think are the advantages and disadvantages of family working in the business?

The business started out as a hobby for Annemarie with solid support from her husband. Her sons growing up were a great help. Now they are not involved as they both work separately in different agricultural enterprises, and both are willing to help with agricultural advice. She states that it is not a family business, but she would be happy to run it as one if the opportunity arose. If one of her sons chose to take over the running of the lavender business or changing it in some way to accommodate their own agricultural enterprise, she would be very happy. As one of her sons operates his intensive farming business next door growing heirloom vegetables (those grown from seeds handed down from one generation to the next) there could be an opening there for a retail outlet together with hospitality. The infrastructure is already in place. Time will tell.

- *Advantages*: Of family working together: on-hand, understand the enterprise
- *Disadvantages*: Don't like to take orders, have their own way of wanting to do things, too many bosses. All want to be in charge.

FUN FACTS ON: LAVENDER

Lavender (*Scientific Name: Lavandula*) is one of the most fragrant and highly versatile herbs that you can grow. It is used in essential oils, perfumes, in aromatherapy, in traditional herbal medicine and in the kitchen as a culinary herb. Here are some other interesting facts about lavender:

- The name Lavender comes from the Latin verb, "lavare," which means to wash
- Lavender comes from the same family as mint
- Over 2500 years ago, lavender was used in ancient Egypt during the mummification process
- Back in the Elizabethan times, when baths weren't common practice, lavender was used to perfume clothes and bed linen
- The scent of lavender deters mice, flies, mosquitoes and other pests from the area
- Lavender oil can be used to soothe aching muscles and joints, reduce anxiety and stress, and to induce sleep
- It is a commonly used ingredient in potpourri
- Nectar from lavender plants is used to make high quality honey
- In the language of flowers, lavender can mean devotion, luck, success, or happiness
- Lavender plants don't produce seeds; propagation is done by cutting or root divisions
- Most lavender plants are blue or purple, but there are some varieties that come in pink and yellow

Source: Growdirect (2021)

Greg Quicke

From bushman to star man

INTRODUCTION

Key points from the interview

- "Just wing it". Of course, there are some qualifications to this, i.e. attention to detail and processes.
- Be prepared to adjust and be open to learning. There will be some dead-ends, and that is ok and is part of the learning.
- Keep walking and watch the waves. That puts the little things into context
- Greg says like any other business it is all about connecting with people.

Greg Quicke

Transitioned from mechanic to bushman then meditation and it all eventually morphed together into his Astro tours business. He loves to tell his audience: Let's go and watch the earth turn away from the part of the sky that the sun is in.

Further information

- *https://www.astrotours.net/*

Category

Lifestyle / Small business Entrepreneur: According to Bond Collective (2021) a lifestyle entrepreneur is a person who creates a business with the purpose of altering their personal lifestyle. ... A lifestyle entrepreneur focuses more on the life rewards (rather than the monetary rewards) provided to those that have a true passion for their work and enjoy what they're doing.

Small business entrepreneur – Also see Himalee (Interview 3). People interested in small business entrepreneurship are most likely to make a profit that supports their family and a modest lifestyle. They aren't seeking large-scale profits or venture capital funding. Small business entrepreneurship is often when a person owns and runs their own business.

I. KEY DATES

- 1979: James Cook University Marine Biology, Townsville, Queensland. Academic study not for him and decided to go diving instead.
- 1982: Broome, Western Australia. Pearl diver.
- 1983: Alice Springs, Northern Territory. Mechanic at Santa Teresa Mission.
- 1984 - 1997 Broome, Western Australia. Diesel mechanic. Diesel fitter, motorcycle mechanic, road train operator,

bulldozer operator, grader operator, speedway racer of 500 cc methanol burning solo bikes and 1000 cc sidecars. This work often took Greg out of Broome and into the wilder parts of the Kimberley region of Western Australia where standard sleeping arrangements are a swag under the stars. The only roof available and the only one needed for most of the year, was the Milky Way. Greg didn't know anything about stars when he started although like anybody else, he was easily captivated with wonder and awe at the incredibly beautiful star scapes of the Kimberley.

- 1993 – 1995: Broome, The Relaxation Centre. Greg got to figuring things out again and started tuning in to the movements of the earth travelling through space. This really fascinated him, and the internal workings of a Harley V-twin motorbike started to look a bit too easy. He bought a telescope. It was big. Everyone wanted to look in it. He started talking, thinking that he was saying things that everyone already knew. "Keep talking" was the response, so after a few years of encouragement from friends, fellow business colleagues and interested corporate and individual customers, he started Astro Tours in July of 1995. Greg says when people ask him how he came up with the idea, he says the idea came up with him.
- 1995 to the present in Broome: Astronomer, bottle washer and lifter of heavy things. at Greg Quicke's Astro Tours[8] (Astronomy shows). The rest is history and Astro Tours continues to delight people in powerful yet simple ways while providing him with the means to continue sharing the simple insights that still pour into his head. Presenting to school groups, corporate groups and to amazingly switched-on groups of people who come together seemingly at random to join his regular shows. Greg is still riding motor bikes, surfing, gardening, chi gung (a form of Chinese gentle exercise) on Cable Beach in the mornings and meditating in rhythm with the moon cycle. Amidst the chaos, the stars and planets are regular and display an amazing synchronicity, harmony and resonance with each other. Greg says, "It seems to me that everything is exactly in its right place, having exactly the right relationships with

[8] *https://www.facebook.com/astrotoursbroome/*

exactly the right timings so it may be worth considering that we are too". Astro Tours runs with around 6 staff and training takes up to 6 months. He also has volunteers work for the company. Sometimes the volunteers become staff. Many of the volunteers are actually qualified scientists or student Astrophysicists. The universities don't teach the practical understanding of the sky and use his training to round out their studies.

Authors' note: One of the authors had heard of Greg so when he was in Broome in 2019, he made sure to see the show and say hello. No doubt amongst 8,000 visitors per year Greg may not have remembered him but Greg's passion left an impression on the author who made a mental note to contact Greg again at some time.

II. GETTING TO KNOW THE PERSON

1. What is success?

Greg sees this as being able to help fellow humanity, and to add value to their lives.

2. What is your favourite TV show, movie or book and why?

- TV: Greg does not have a TV.
- Movie: He watches the occasional movie – he liked the storyline in *Avatar*.
- Books: Greg reads a lot of books on philosophy, science and meditation.

3. What are your hobbies and/or Interests?

He still likes his motorcycles, riding and working on them. He surfs and kitesurfs.

Figure 44 - Daniel, Cyril and Greg, August 2021

III. TIPS

4. How did you get through your worst times?

Greg says the solution to all our problems in life is to walk on the beach and sleep under the stars. "Keep walking and watch the waves. That puts the little things into context".

5. What keeps you awake at night?

Nothing! He sleeps like a baby.

6. What are your typical daily routines?

Greg gets up with daylight. He walks to Cable beach, does his exercises, has a swim and then back home for breakfast and then into work. His work depends on whether there is a show on that night. He used to run shows 4 to 6 nights but over the years has worked out that 3 nights per week with an increased capacity is more efficient. The show runs between two and two and a half hours. It takes one and a half hours to set up, so he starts at 2 pm, sometimes collecting his crew. All the equipment is stored in a 40-foot container. He feels that the great thing about the show is that it is different every night. After the end of the show all staff must lie on the ground, and no one can get up until everyone has seen a shooting star (a small piece of rock or dust that hits Earth's atmosphere from space and incinerates). Greg noted this should only take around 10 minutes. Greg then goes home and in bed by 10 or 11pm on worknights. Earlier for non-working nights.

7. What advice would you give yourself starting out?

Greg says, "just wing it". Of course, there are some qualifications to this, that is, attention to detail and processes which are part of the learning. Be prepared to adjust and be open to learning. There will be some dead-end work and that is ok and part of the learning.

IV. BUSINESS CASE EXAMPLES

8. Provide a case you managed well and why?

Greg started the business in small steps. While working and sleeping under the stars he slowly realised he had a talent for understanding and explaining what was happening in the sky. He purchased one telescope for himself with no idea that telescopes would become the new tools of his trade. A few years later after some considerable encouragement from anyone who he happened to share some stars with, (get on with it!) he sent "flyers" around. Within two weeks he was working 7 nights per week. The business was successful right from the start. The key was looking after the guests and his staff are very attentive to the needs of customers.

Authors' note: The Author remembers the staff assistance in helping find Venus, and more importantly getting their famous hot chocolate and home-made Anzac bikkies. Then he bought the book and T-shirt!

A few years ago, Greg relocated to a property which he now rents and has put some infrastructure on it (seating etc).

In 1995 he was running three different types of shows:

- 2 to 2.5 hour shows running for 6 to 7 months of year (dry season)
- Overnight stargazing dinner with a small group
- 3- 4-day desert Outback Stargazing Adventure trip

He ultimately realised that only the first type of show provided the best return for the effort and has continued on with this one, dropping the others.

In the wet off season, Greg will do corporate presentations as a keynote or guest speaker in Perth, Sydney, Melbourne, Brisbane, Adelaide, Darwin as well as regional and outback events, when travel was a thing. He has presented overseas including recent trips to Italy including the Vatican Observatory and as guest speaker at USA events.

Greg also presents on television for the BBC and the ABC:

- *https://www.bbc.co.uk/programmes/p04xx7x3*
- *https://iview.abc.net.au/show/stargazing-live/series/1/video/DO1616H001S00*
- *https://www.abc.net.au/catalyst/greg--quicke/13184962*
- *https://www.abc.net.au/tveducation/programs/stargazers-guide-to-the-cosmos/12137104* and for example see *https://iview.abc.net.au/video/DO1704W001S00*

9. Provide a case that did not go well and why?

Case 1 - Weather

The weather has been the only major issue. Most of the time the sky is clear in Broome but occasionally it gets cloudy. Greg evaluates this possibility before the show and will cancel (very rare – due to the amount of paperwork required it takes twice as long to cancel a show as to run one!). If it does get cloudy, he will still talk about the sky and pretend it is clear. The audiences generally approve of this. Greg tells the story of one time it got very overcast, and Greg offered refunds to the guests. Everyone refused the refund, with one exception. There has been an interesting mix of guests over the years. One time a guest insisted on seeing Jupiter. Greg had to advise him that Jupiter was not in the sky that night, as it was on the other side of the Earth. The guest couldn't understand or accept this. Greg says like any other business it is all about connecting with people.

Case 2 Other sites

Greg has tried other sites for his Astro Tours show. He spent 4 seasons on the South coast of Western Australia and 4 seasons at Rottnest Island near Perth.

These sites had clear skies but were too cold at night. These other sites, whilst not great financially, did help him put Astro Tours on the map. As a result, he has focused on the Broome site, where he happens to live.

10. What conclusions can be drawn by comparing these cases?

Greg says the cases reflect that you just need to wing it, with preparation and be prepared to improvise and make changes as needed.

11. What cultural issues did you experience? How were they overcome? How is Australia different? Were these cases affected by.

Greg notes that during the white Australia policy period (1901 Act that effectively stopped all non-European immigration) Broome was effectively exempt. *https://broomemuseum.org.au/race-rights-rivalries/white-australia/*. With interracial marriage this made Broome into a melting pot of cultures that still exist today. This means today everyone is welcome and there is a great feeling of acceptance of all cultures. As a result, he experiences no particular cultural issues.

V. VOLATILITY (FOR EXAMPLE COVID)

12. How has the virus affected your business?

COVID-19 has not, in general, had a great impact on his business in Broome. While tourism business is down from the Eastern states, there is plenty of business to be had from Western Australia to keep going. They have a lot of "regulars" that keep coming back.

Authors' note: Both Authors will be there ASAP after lockdown ends!

13. What lasting impact do you think it will have on your business?

Greg has not had to make any changes to the business so no lasting impact.

14. What have you learned from it that you will now implement in your business?

Greg says it has become apparent that you need to be on your toes, ready for anything.

VI. FAMILY BUSINESS

15. Are you in a family business and from your experience what do you think are the advantages and disadvantages of family working in the business?

Greg says his business is not a family business. He wouldn't mind his daughter, Elizabeth coming in, but she has other interests (see below photo). He doesn't have a view on family businesses.

Figure 45 - Greg and daughter Elizabeth who finished the course in Marine Biology that Greg started and didn't finish

FUN FACTS ON: TELEVISION

- *Television won't last because people will soon get tired of staring at a plywood box every night.* **Darryl Zanuck, movie producer, 20th Century Fox 1946**
- *"Our people are becoming less literate by the minute," the writer lamented, suggesting that in the zero-sum game of recreational hours, TV would eat up more and more of the time people once spent reading books and thinking thoughts. "By the 21st Century our people doubtless will be squint-eyed, hunchbacked and fond of the dark," the writer predicted.* **TIME magazine 1951**
- *I will never understand why they cook on TV. I can't smell it, can't eat it, can't taste it. The end of the show they hold it up to the camera: "Well, here it is. You can't have any. Goodbye.".* **Jerry Seinfeld**
- *Television is like the invention of indoor plumbing. It didn't change people's habits. It just kept them inside the house.* **Alfred Hitchcock**
- *Television is not real life. In real life people actually have to leave the coffee shop and go to jobs.* **Bill Gates**
- *I don't watch television; I think it destroys the art of talking about oneself.* **Stephen Fry, English writer and actor**

James Barbour

From selling cucumbers to pickling them

INTRODUCTION

Key points from the interview

- Getting input from others is useful for gaining another perspective.
- He would advise not to worry about failing. Some people want to get things perfect, but some things can never be perfect.
- You need to know what you can do and what you can't do.
- The benefit of being professional and sticking to your principles
- There is a difference between "skin in the game" and "soul in the game". The former is where you have a financial interest in the outcome and the latter is where you have personal rewards in addition to financial rewards.

James Barbour

James has always been a pickle person. Growing up in Virginia, USA his mother claims that from as early as age 2, he's been eagerly eating them. He met the love of his life, Liza (from the Mornington Peninsula), whilst volunteering in Tonga and after over a decade in Melbourne, they started a business making American-style dill pickles. They called their business "Dillicious". There has never been a dill moment since then.

Authors' note: That joke has put us into a real pickle

Further information

- *https://dillicious.com.au/pages/about-us*
- *https://dillicious.com.au/*

Category

Young business / start up business entrepreneur. Using Equity crowd funding to give expansion a helping hand.

I. KEY DATES

- Early 2009: James (from Virginia, USA) meets Liza (from the Mornington Peninsula, Victoria, Australia) whilst volunteering in the Kingdom of Tonga.
- Late 2009: James and Liza moved to Melbourne, Australia – where Liza grew up.
- 2013: Married
- 2017: James' life is going pretty great: happily married raising two children on Victoria's picturesque Mornington Peninsula. Except there's just one thing missing: pickles. There's a pickle shaped hole in his heart. From imports to imposters, James and Liza sought out alternatives but nothing could fill the void, and in that moment, Dillicious was born. In the absence of a worthy pickle came the inspiration to make their own. Liza maintains her long-standing tenure at Monash University as a lecturer and PhD candidate in public health nutrition and sustainable food systems. Backed by over 18 years of experience in hospitals, community health centres and not-for-profits, Liza is also an Advanced Accredited Practicing Dietitian and proud member of the Dietitians Australia and the Public Health Association of Australia. In order to satisfy James' cravings for pickles, Liza did her research sourcing out the best she could get her hands on and sampling them with her pickle-crazed counterpart. But it wasn't until they experimented with making their own did she realise just how good pickles could be…the crunch, the tang, the flavour- and good for you too! What's not to love?
- Late 2018: Dillicious sold their first jar of pickles at the Mt Eliza Farmers' Market. They grossly under-estimated the demand and had to re-stock their stall twice. Over the next couple of months, they amplified weekend production with the help of many friends and family. They booked more and more markets until their weekends were filled to the brim with production and market stalls.
- May 2019: James resigned from his full-time corporate sales job to work on Dillicious full time. It was only one week later that Australia's largest distributor of gourmet cheese and specialty foods picked them up for National

distribution. The stars were aligned and at that moment the small family business took a giant step to becoming much more. They have continued to work around the clock to grow the business, signed on major retailers such as Costco warehouses Australia-wide and national restaurant groups such as Rando Sando (found in every Strike Bowling, Sky Zone, Holey Moley Golf, Archie Brothers) and Australian Venues Co. (one of Australia's largest and fastest growing hospitality groups). All while remaining true to the vision to keep it local, push Australian produce and maintain quality production to deliver the ultimate crunchiness. They are on a journey to redefine the humble dill pickle for Australians.

Authors' note: It's been a jarring experience, (sorry the authors are just a couple of Dills)

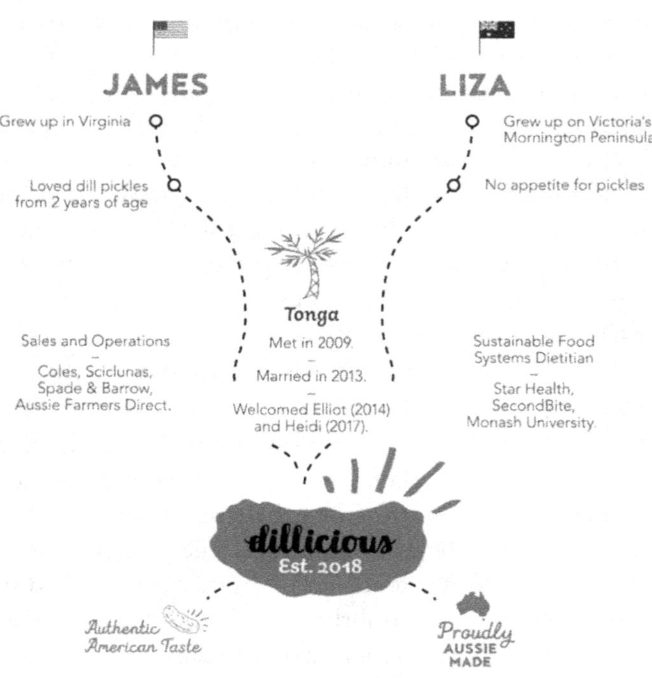

Figure 46 - The delicious Dillicious Journey chart

- 2021: Dillicious completed a fundraise through the relatively new area of Equity Crowd Funding (ECF). ECF is a way to buy shares in private companies and is typically used for investments in early-stage start-ups. It is similar to regular crowd funding but with a key difference – people buy shares in companies that list projects, not their goods or services. About $250,000 was raised with the help of Birchal (see *https://www.birchal.com/company/dillicious*). The funds received have enabled them to:
    - Streamline production processes by purchasing manufacturing equipment
    - Expand production capacity by moving into a custom-built facility – The Brinery (September 2021)
    - Expand their product offering (Brine infused condiments)
    - Increase demand through targeted marketing
- James says that they consider their equity raise as successful although believe a greater investment in Public Relations (PR) Strategy would have seen a much greater fund raise.

Authors' note: maybe for the next fund raise

- The average investment was just over $1,000 although many invested a few hundred dollars and quite a few were $10,000+. James said this is a very interesting area of obtaining finance and great care must be taken to get the marketing and statements about risk and financial projections right. It makes for an interesting comparison to alternative options such as Angel investors, venture capital and to debt finance.

Authors' note: Further information on Equity Crowd Funding see the Sources of Funds section.

II. GETTING TO KNOW THE PERSON

1. What is success?

James sees business success in simple terms – he likes to see happy smiling customers and seeing the product in people's hands.

2. What is your favourite TV show, movie or book and why?

- TV: *The Project* and AFL.
- Book: His favourite book is the *"The Great Gatsby"*. I love the idea of the person with everything still not being fulfilled and all he wanted was the love of his life.
- Movie: *"Legends of the Fall"* (1994 movie about 3 brothers and their father living in the wilderness of Montana in the early 1900s)

3. What are your hobbies and/or Interests?

These days, outside of business, his interests revolve around his family, his wife and children. He has built up a passion for AFL and follows the Sydney Swans. He advises that it did take him a little time to work out the rules.

Authors' note: good luck with that!

III. TIPS

4. How did you get through your worst times?

James believes getting helpful input from others is useful for getting another perspective. James shares both the good things as well as problems with his family and friends and he finds that this gives him great support, without overburdening them. The key is to get the right balance in life.

5. What keeps you awake at night?

Not a lot keeps him awake at night as he is a sound sleeper. Sometimes if something is on his mind it might motivate him to get up early to address the issue.

6. What are your typical daily routines?

James is an early riser, waking between 4 - 4.30 AM and usually reads the news with a coffee for 15 minutes. That is the only time he reads the news to avoid getting distracted. He will then check his emails in case any calls are needed early. James is then off to the warehouse for 9 to 10 hours, but Liza and James make sure the family has dinner together every night at 5.30 to 6 pm. Then he has time with his wife, Liza to watch the news or a TV show. He and Liza have a dedicated 'business meeting' a couple of evenings a week, with an agenda. As a husband-wife team they believe this is important to contain their Dillicious chat so that it doesn't dominate their family time. While James will check his emails approximately hourly during the working day, he doesn't let email control his schedule.

7. What advice would you give yourself starting out?

He would advise himself not to worry about failing. Some people want to get things perfect, but some things can never be perfect. James says sometimes you can overthink issues and the key is to decide and then implement.

IV. BUSINESS CASE EXAMPLES

8. Provide a case you managed well and why?

A national retail chain contacted Dillicious as they were interested in their product. This was their first really large customer that came to them directly rather via their distributor. The customer loved their product, but price and distribution were questioned. James was politely firm on their pricing and preference for using his existing distribution partner. The customer agreed to James's terms and because of the introduction to James's distributor, went on to source additional products from their gourmet cheese range.

9. Provide a case that did not go well and why?

When James first started the business, his distributor lined up a particular customer for James to supply. Dillicious started production based on verbal projected orders and had three weeks' stock ready to supply. The customer did not complete the order due to pricing issues. It took James many months to sell the stock to alternative customers. It was a very stressful period.

10. What conclusions can be drawn by comparing these cases?

The main lesson from the above cases is the old saying "you need to know what you can do and what you can't do". The benefit of being professional and sticking to your principles was clearly of benefit in Question 8. In question 9 there are some cases where you may produce without an order, depending on the Industry you are in and even more importantly, after you have developed a trusting relationship with the other party. In this case that had not yet been developed. If you share your information and explain and communicate it clearly, as in question 8, you may be surprised at how people will be willing to assist. James sees that many people get into trouble by not being assertive on what is right for their business. This puts themselves under pressure and leaves them exposed when external volatility such as the COVID-19 pandemic occurs.

11. What cultural issues did you experience? How were they overcome? How is Australia different? Were these cases affected by.

James said his US accent does raise some questions and thinks it is a net positive. Apart from that, he fits in to a fairly expected "look" of Australian business people, so he has had no real surprises.

He does find it interesting to compare business culture in Australia and USA and finds in many areas the US is ahead in strategy.

> **Authors' note:** see discussion on Equity Fund raising in the chapter on Sources of Finance, where Australia has been 5 to 10 years behind USA. For further information on Equity Crowd Funding see the Sources of Funds section in the final chapter of the book that contain this, and the other 14 interviews.

V. VOLATILITY (FOR EXAMPLE COVID)

12. How has the virus affected your business?

James says the business sells via different distribution channels, but ultimately most of his end customers are restaurants, food courts and other food stores. In March 2020 many businesses closed due to the pandemic and Dillicious dropped 80% in turnover. Also, markets were closed, meaning that stream of direct sales was completely paused. Whilst markets were never a large proportion of profit, they served (and continue to serve) an important role in getting the Dillicious name out there. During the pandemic, retail sales increased whilst food service declined. There was a big roller-coaster ride during and between lockdowns.

13. What lasting impact do you think it will have on your business?

James says the need to be ready for volatility has obviously become more crucial. James thinks that the USA does business strategy generally really well and possibly better than Australians who tend to think in more straightforward ways. Global supply chains are clearly a major risk area. Wherever possible, James has long preferred to deal with local suppliers and this is now working in their favour. Consumers are becoming more aware than ever of the quality and source of product so Dillicious' commitment to source their ingredients locally has been a real point of difference. It is James' opinion that retailers (including Coles and Woolworths) will be driven by consumer demand so as consumers become more aware of these benefits, retailers will respond.

14. What have you learned from it that you will now implement in your business?

James said that Dillicious will remain true to their values while rolling with the punches. James said he and Liza genuinely enjoy thinking outside of the box so when faced with a challenge, they get their heads together and come up with a few plans. They learnt early on, and particularly through their involvement in Monash University's Generator program, that it's always a good idea to reach out to people with a diverse range of perspectives and skill sets. So, they run their ideas past various people who they consider much smarter than themselves!

VI. FAMILY BUSINESS

15. Are you in a family business and from your experience what do you think are the advantages and disadvantages of family working in the business?

Yes, James thinks that his is a family business, even with 240 shareholders (through the Equity fundraising). He loves that the whole family is involved, and the kids enjoy and respect the nature of the pickle business. He provided the following comparative information:

- Advantages of family business include:
  - The ability to make decisions based on "gut" feel rather than having to justify every decision with onerous spreadsheets and risk analyses
  - Having the kids involved in many aspects of the business – they come to markets and the Brinery and see first-hand just how hard James and Liza work
- Disadvantages of family business include:
  - James sees that family business members are fully responsible for every decision
  - There is never an "off" button

- There's a blurry line between business and personal matters – setting up processes to keep this line clearer is critical

James sees a difference between "skin in the game", where the reward is a financial interest, and "soul in the game", where the rewards are not only financial but involves other personal rewards as well.

Figure 47 - Chief taste-testers: Elliot and Heidi

FUN FACTS ON: PICKLES

The Facts:

A pickled cucumber (commonly known as a pickle in the United States and Canada or generically as gherkins in the United Kingdom) is a cucumber that has been pickled in a brine, vinegar, or other solution and left to ferment for a period of time, by either immersing the cucumbers in an acidic solution or through souring by lacto-fermentation.

The fun part:

- Pickles have been around since ancient times, although there is some disagreement as to when exactly in history people started eating them. Some believe the first pickle was created in Mesopotamia in 2400 B.C.E. Others believe it was as early as 2030 B.C.E.
- The phrase "in a pickle" was first introduced by Shakespeare in his play, The Tempest. The quotes read, "How cam'st thou in this pickle?" and "I have been in such a pickle"
- November 14th is National Pickle Day.
- Cleopatra ate pickles because she believed they were one of the things that helped her stay beautiful.
- Approximately 100,000 to 125,000 acres (about 400 to 500 square kilometres) are devoted to growing pickling cucumbers in the United States.
- In the U.S., pickles are made in 30 of the 50 states with Michigan and North Carolina making the most pickles.
- Kool-Aid pickles are made by soaking dill pickles in strong Kool-Aid and are very popular in parts of Mississippi.
- A town in Michigan that claims to be the Christmas Pickle Capital of the World holds an annual pickle parade led by the Grand Dillmeister.
- You can hear the crunch of a good pickle at 10 paces.
- According to the U.S. Supreme Court, pickles are technically a "fruit" of the vine (like tomatoes), but they are generally known as a vegetable.

- During WWII the U.S. Government tagged 40 percent of all pickle production for the ration kits of the armed forces.
- Americans consume more than 9 pounds (about 4 kg) of pickles per person annually.
- In Connecticut in order for a pickle to officially be considered a pickle, it must bounce. (provided by Austin Greenwood)

Source: Mobile-Cuisine (2021)

Part B:

Discussion and Analysis

In this part there are two sections:

- B1 Analysis of Interviews
- B2 Summary Information.

Analysis of Interviews

INTRODUCTION

The interviews were broken into a number of parts, and below we will discuss each in detail:

I. Key dates
II. Getting to know the person
III. Tips
IV. Business case examples
V. Volatility for example COVID-19
VI. Family business

I. KEY DATES

In each interview we looked at the key dates. From them we could see that some interviewees were serial entrepreneurs (for example Alice and Phillip, Interview 6), or others were accidental entrepreneurs, that is they entered into business by accident (Annemarie Manders, Interview 13) and they have stayed there. Our only intrapreneur is Greg Whateley (Interview 7). He left a secure university position to work for himself in the music composition industry and after four months of zero income he thought it was wiser to return to paid employment. From his interview you will see that he became a very successful intrapreneur.

Figure 48 - Emptying the piggy bank

The many employers of Greg Whateley have been very fortunate that his piggy bank ran out of money. Otherwise, he would have started his own business.

He has contributed greatly to the organisations that he worked for. Both authors know this very well.

II. GETTING TO KNOW THE PERSON

1. What is success?

As expected, we received a wide variety of responses. Some saw success only in terms of business (for example Warrier in Interview 1) whereas some were looking at a simpler view, including happiness and personal achievement (for example John Engelander, Interview 4). To us, this indicates that a pre-conceived view of success is not particularly critical as a motivator for business success.

Making lots of money was not a feature of any of our respondents. Alice and Philip (Interview 6) capture the general mood – being able to spend $500 without worrying and celebrate the little things, for example, a new customer.

2. What is your favourite TV show, movie or book and why?

The answers to this question provided an interesting insight into the culture and tastes of our interviewees. We received a very wide series of responses reflecting the range of general community tastes.

We saw a variety of movies such as Hitchcock, Bollywood, Hurricane, and Avatar and a couple liked the Sound of music. As for television there were crime dramas, Seinfeld, Yes Minister, News and documentaries. There were a huge variety of books ranging from fantasy, philosophy, fiction, non-fiction. Notable books were The Violinist from Venice and The Fourth Estate.

3. What are your hobbies and/or Interests?

A few of our respondents saw their work as their main interest (for example Alice and Phillip, Interview 6, and Greg Whateley, Interview 7). To some extent this question depends on what is happening with the person at the time in their life and their hobbies or interest may change over time. Many respondents expressed the importance of regular physical activity, for example cycling (Robert Roshan, Interview 8), walking, sport, Surfing (Greg Quicke, Interview 14), on their overall well-being. Himalee Karunasena (Interview 3) is heavily involved in community and voluntary activities, and Greg Whateley (Interview 7) collects wine.

Everyone needs hobbies and interests to break from work, otherwise it all gets too much.

Figure 49 - All too much

III. TIPS

4. How did you get through your worst times?

Most respondents were typified by Robert Roshan (Interview 8) who advised of the need to keep perspective and not be affected by relatively small issues. James Barbour (Interview 15) says getting helpful input from trusted others is useful to get the right perspective.

Margaret Harmer (Interview 9), who was in a position worse than most due to the death of a child in a major car accident in which she and her husband survived, said obtaining support from people who had been through similar events was important. Matija Squire's (Interview 10) motto is "Your circumstances should never dictate your potential". She also had the guidance and support of her father when she was young which turned her life around, which was that it was up to Matija to make her own decisions in life, and her father would support her in whatever she chose to do. John Engelander (Interview 4) says "difficult times do not build character, they reveal it"

5. What keeps you awake at night?

Again, our respondents are all pretty relaxed and not much keeps them up at night. Art Phillips (Interview 5) feels he does tend to worry a little and gets frustrated when others have not followed up but generally sleeps well. Alan Manly (Interview 11) says that after all these years he still worries about cash flow. Matija Squire (Interview 10) feels that she sometimes overthinks issues but practices calm reading and music to calm. Similarly, Himalee (Interview 3) emphasises the need to switch off and give herself space and feels that her Buddhist meditation is of great benefit. When it comes to business issues that keep him awake Robert Roshan (Interview 8) he says that if you are staying awake at night after 25 years in business, perhaps you should consider other ways of earning a dollar. Warrier (Interview 1) watches cricket.

Authors' note: speaking from experience this is a sure way to get to sleep.

6. What are your typical daily routines?

As expected, most of the respondents' work schedule dominates their daily routines, for example with emails and meetings. Some try to allow for private family time, for example James Barbour (Interview 15) tries to schedule work discussion with his wife, Liza, at set times, especially at home so as not to overtake family time at home. Others try to work in some exercise (Greg Quick, Interview 14). Greg lives on the Western Australian coast in Broome, and has a great routine: he walks from home to Cable Beach, exercises, swims, prepares for his show, checks emails and work issues. Annemarie Manders (Interview 13) in her own way has a similar routine. She believes in getting up early and working when fresh, exercises breakfast goes through her tasks and emails. On the other hand, John Engelander (Interview 4) and Matija Squire (Interview 10) do not follow any set routine outside of certain scheduled commitments.

7. What advice would you give yourself starting out?

Almost all respondents said that they would advise their younger self to "have a go" but be a little careful along the way. Jon Tse (Interview 12) almost without hesitation said that one needs to be prepared to make every mistake in the book. Art Phillips (Interview 5) recommends that one enjoys the moment and do it with passion. Margaret Harmer (Interview 9) and Greg Whateley (Interview 7) both advise to be careful not to let work overwhelm your life. In Question 6 of his interview Greg Whateley stated that he likes to relay to young people his "spinning plates" metaphor on running a successful business. This is where an entertainer spins multiple plates and doesn't attend to them until the entertainer sees that one needs assistance. Greg has adopted this as a key way he manages people. Himalee Karunasena (Interview 3) says due diligence is vital but so is your gut feel and you need to do your homework so that people will not take advantage of you. Warrier (Interview 1) says something similar to this in that you need to temper the passion with commerciality and regularly check your cash flow and financial statements. Alan Many (Interview 11) agrees, as the owner of a business of substance, he knows the importance of cashflow. We will further consider gut feel in Question 9, below

Many of the interviewees spoke about perseverance and not giving up. They agree that it is also about working smarter rather than just harder. Here is a quotation on this matter from **Steve Jobs**, Co-founder, CEO, Chairman Apple Inc, who said *"I'm convinced that about half of what separates the successful entrepreneurs from the non-successful ones is pure perseverance."*

IV. BUSINESS CASE EXAMPLES

8. Provide a case you managed well and why?

This is where we start to see why the 15 entrepreneurs selected have been successful. None have done anything so extraordinary that they have been awarded major prizes. There is no magic, or bull sh*t (BS), but it is just plain good business practices that got them where they are.

Figure 50 - No BS here

Authors' note: while there may have been a bit of occasional BS here and there, from what we can see it was only incidental.

We would like to point out a few of the interviewees' successes:

- Art Phillips (Interview 5) selecting good professional agents (sub -publishers) to represent him.
- Greg Whateley (Interview 7) using his experience, and that of key people, to build a business quietly but cleverly.
- Robert Roshan (Interview 8) looking after his customers and the needs of the customers of his customers.
- Margaret Harmer (Interview 9) obtaining support and a good PR person to find a solution to a need.
- James Barbour (Interview 15) staying professional with his customers.

Where adjustments were needed, they were quickly done:

- Alan Manly (Interview 11) reducing the range of campuses when costs were blowing out; and
- Greg Quicke (Interview 14) reducing his offer of shows to what he could make a reasonable return from.

When the synergies are right, a combination of quick response and experience, can result in the introduction of a new product:

- John Engelander (Interview 4) with Ecobin
- Rahul Daga (Interview 2) with his Tennis Australia racquet tags.

Sometimes some deft work to respond to an unexpected surge of demand or need within the business can produce results:

- Warrier (Interview 1) managing a sudden surge in business
- Himalee Karunasena (Interview 3) with the books and gifts to Sri Lankan refugees
- Alice and Philip (Interview 6) responding to a supermarket order with due care
- Matija Squire (Interview 10) being at the right place and at the right time for a client in Japan
- Jon Tse (Interview 12) with hand sanitiser during the COVID-19 pandemic

- Annemarie (Interview 13) being able to present at multiple festivals at the same time.

Remember this famous quotation: *"Success has many owners; failure is an orphan."*, **John Kennedy**

9. Provide a case that did not go well and why?

In some ways this may be the most important question as we know that as humans, we all make mistakes. As can be expected every businessperson will make many errors. The key is to minimise their likelihood and consequence. **Jessica Herrin**, founder and CEO of Stella & Dot a retailer of ladies clothing, jewellery and handbags) said it well when she said, *"You have to see failure as the beginning and the middle, but never entertain it as an end."*

A client of substance of one of the authors never admitted to making a mistake. One day the businessperson said s/he had made a big error. The author was shocked! What was the error? The businessperson said the error was placing faith in an employee who made an error! It is important to note that as this business person aged many significant mistakes were made almost destroying that person's business, however, this person never admitted to making a mistake, except for the one above.

It is interesting that business plans, whilst important, cannot consider all risk factors and this is where "gut- feel" (or intuition) comes in, which is really about using good observation and experience. A number of interviewees spoke about the need to be very aware of gut feel: Himalee (Interview 3), Jon (Interview 12) and James (Interview 15). The following **Kevin Rose** (who co-founded of the American news aggregator Digg) quotation is very relevant: *"Don't let others convince you that the idea is good when your gut tells you it's bad."*

Often the business model is good but local conditions can cause a problem. For example:

- Sudhir Warrier (Interview 1) with the cruise ship in Queensland with unexpected local antipathy

- Rahul Daga (Interview 2) with employees in the second franchise he took over
- Greg Whateley (Interview 7) with the Japanese local culture regarding lengthy and detailed Western commercial contracts
- Annemarie Manders (Interview 13) under-estimating weed control
- Greg Quicke (Interview 14) with the local weather in Perth.

Finance is of course one of the big issues as Margaret Harmer (Interview 9) found out with the loss of government funding for her not for profit organisation.

Rapid expansion caused difficulties in managing costs is a related financial issue:

- Alice and Philip (Interview 6) taking on the supermarket order but without the negotiating ability of big supplier
- Robert Roshan (Interview 8) taking on a new company
- Jon Tse (Interview 12) with the early days of Zookai.

Perhaps one of the biggest issues and one in which one of the authors has had some experience is in choosing the wrong business partner to work with. The business partner needs to have similar ethics and values otherwise it is going to be a problem just waiting to occur (as can be seen in the below cartoon). Trust issues are vital as was seen with:

- John Engelander (Interview 4) with partners in a couple of start-ups.
- Art Phillips (Interview 5) with his business partner
- Matija Squire (Interview 10) with her start-up partner
- James Barbour (Interview 15) trusting a new customer.

Careful who you choose as a business partner. Are you compatible with them?

Figure 51 - Business partners

Sometimes, difficulties can arise when dealing with the bureaucracy in highly regulated businesses, as we saw with:

- Himalee Karunasena (Interview 3) and her petrol station roadworthy registration issues
- Alan Manly (Interview 11) with the Thailand venture.

> **Authors' note:** Alan's Melbourne campus was also caught up in Bureaucracy

10. What conclusions can be drawn by comparing these cases?

Many conclusions can be drawn from our 15 stories of entrepreneurs. Our entrepreneurs made mistakes but fortunately they had sufficient perseverance, resilience and resources to be able to press on. Examples include:

- Robert Roshan (Interview 8) emphasises need to resilience through difficulties. He said that sometimes organic or systematic growth can be better than rushing an expansion
- Margaret Harmer (Interview 9) – said that despite the many significant difficulties when Government funding stopped, she pressed on running operations from her bedroom.
- Alan Manly (Interview 11) – there were many examples in his story, for example the setting up of the Sydney campus versus Thailand campus.

Being careful of where you are in the market and preparation needed:

- Sudhir Warrier (Interview 1) – evaluation of all business risks are important
- Rahul (Interview 2) says you need a Plan B and even a Plan C.
- Himalee Karunasena (Interview 3) – you need to understand local knowledge and if possible, work in the business first before investing.
- Art Phillips (Interview 5) – need to deal with corporate and Indie (independent) organisations differently
- Alice and Philip (Interview 6) –supermarkets and small retailers are set up very differently
- Annemarie (Interview 13) – preparation and research, for example on weed control

Sometimes you just have to persist despite the occasional problem.

- Jon Tse (Interview 12) – says hindsight is a wonderful thing. Make mistakes and learn from them.
- Greg Quicke (Interview 14) – continue to try different things
- James Barbour (Interview 15) – he started with a difficult customer, and this was a learning exercise and now it was just a step in the journey.

Sometimes it is important that you have control because your business partner may not have the same understanding and/or values, for example John Engelander and his aromatherapy partner. See the above cartoon which illustrated the tensions that may arise if here are differing values.

Ultimately, it is really all about dealing with people. This is robustly illustrated by Subroto Bagchi, the co-founder of Mindtree, an Indian multinational information technology and outsourcing company, who said, "Selling is not a pushy, winner-takes-all, macho act. It is an empathy-led, process-driven, and knowledge-intensive discipline. Because, in the end, people buy from people." Examples from our interviews include:

- Matija (Interview 4) – Understanding Japanese people
- Greg Whateley (Interview 4) – Got to be there in person! This applies everywhere (management by walking around), but especially if trying to manage a Japanese campus from Australia.

11. What cultural issues did you experience? How were they overcome? How is Australia different? Were these cases affected by cultural issues?

If the responses from our entrepreneurs are anything to go by Australia seems to be a very egalitarian place. Many of the interviewees, perhaps due to their background, have actually gone out of their way to make people of different cultural backgrounds feel at home. Warier (Interview 1) Robert Roshan (Interview 8), Alan Manly (Interview 11) and Annemarie Manders (Interview 13) are good examples. Greg Quicke (Interview 14) noted that Broome is a real melting pot due to Broome's historical position during the white Australia policy period.

Apart from an isolated incident reported by Himalee Karunasena (Interview 3) against her, there were hardly any issues arose in the 30 + years that she has been in Australia.

A few of our respondents pointed to the issues in understanding overseas cultural differences – Both Greg Whateley (Interview 7) and Matija Squire (Interview 10) had this regarding dealing with Japanese. Matija Squire also pointed out that some countries do not have a culture of working online, Philippines was case in point, and this took some work. Alan Many (Interview 11) pointed out the same thing but with Thailand.

It was interesting that the cultural differences in dealing with small business versus large corporates was pointed out by Art Phillips (Interview 5) and Alice and Phillip (Interview 6). Jon Tse (Interview 12) and James Barbour (Interview 15) noted some different business attitudes between USA and Australia.

V. VOLATILITY (FOR EXAMPLE COVID)

12. How has the virus affected your business?

This question really relates to general volatility but in the midst of the biggest world pandemic for a century the focus understandability is on COVID-19. Naturally, apart from several of our respondents, all our entrepreneurs have been dramatically affected, in some cases threatening the entire business. Jobkeeper was of some benefit last year but not for everyone and certainly not in late 2021.

Robert Roshan (Interview 8) noted the wide-ranging physical and mental stress on his staff and being able to provide services to customers. Luckily, he has good staff and customers which should help his company navigate through the pandemic.

It is probably easier to note the few businesses not particularly affected:

- Alice and Philip's (Interview 6) pet food business was an "excepted" business (care of animals), so they only had relatively minor disruptions due to COVID-19 restrictions including some staffing issues
- Greg Quicke (Interview 14) in Broome said that even with interstate and overseas tourism business being down he has maintained constant business from local Western Australian tourism.

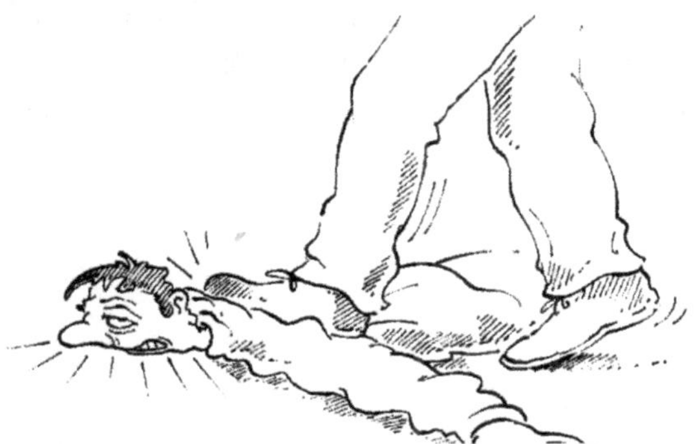

Figure 52 - Is volatility (including COVID-19) squashing you and your business?

13. What lasting impact do you think it will have on your business?

This question relates also to Question 14, in that the below responses tend to indicate the actions taken will probably last for a long time.

- Sudhir Warrier (Interview 1) sees COVID-19, as part of volatility, and as a wakeup call and that businesses need to be better prepared. They need to review their operations and resources regularly.
- Rahul Daga (Interview 2) has a business providing printing for the education industry. He is confident that while some training will continue as a hybrid delivery (online and in person), there will be demand for his printing services as more face-to-face events return.
- Greg Whateley (Interview 7) has instigated at UBSS a heavy investment in technology to give the students a real-life face-to-face on-line experience. This was happening at some level previously but has accelerated during COVID-19 pandemic.
- Robert Roshan (Interview 8) states that while his staff are working online and probably will continue to do so to some extent, it is far less efficient that working collaboratively face to face.
- Matija Squire (Interview 10) said there will be more uncertainty in business for the foreseeable future and contracts will need to allow for this. She has been fortunate to have consistent work.
- Annemarie Manders (Interview 13) is hoping there will not be any lasting effects and that people will be keen to get back to visiting farms and gardens. In the meantime, she must manage her costs carefully.

14. What have you learned from it that you will now implement in your business?

The COVID-19 pandemic clearly affected our entrepreneurs as much as anyone in the community. Everyone has been affected, and many reported the impact makes them appreciate what we have a little more.

Figure 53 - Being managerially effective in these high-pressure volatile (including COVID-19 related) times

In relation to their business, our interviewees have generally been quick and responsive to learn from the experience and look for ways to keep their business going. Some examples are:

Working more online is naturally going to increase:

- Himalee Karunasena (Interview 3) is always looking at being creative and looking at ways to make her businesses more efficient.
- Greg Whateley (Interview 7) has published numerous articles on the continuing shift to on-line learning. See his views on technology in previous question.
- Alan Manly (Interview 11) similarly sees the future as adapting to flexible styles of learning

- John Tse (Interview 12) says the pandemic means there are no rules. He has looked at alternative distribution channels
- James Barbour (Interview 15) mentioned the need to keep networking and keep getting advice.

Many of our interviewees spoke about focusing on things that they can control:

- Rahul likewise (Interview 2) says businesses will have to reinvent ways to cope with the changed circumstances and engage with their customers' needs.
- John Engelander (Interview 4) says you need to keep evaluating options and be ready for challenges and opportunities.
- Matija Squire (Interview 10) says we must sometimes accept a less than optimal result due to things being outside of our control.
- Annemarie (Interview 13) says we need access to spare working capital and being vigilant on COVID-19 safe practices in the long term.

Some have built risk management into their business:

- Sudhir Warrier (Interview 1) like Robert Roshan (Interview 8) has high labour costs and this needs to be carefully managed.
- Art Phillips (Interview 5) says a drop in income emphasises the need to keep looking for new options and you should not be afraid to look at new ideas.
- Alice and Philip (Interview 6) are always ready to adapt to changed circumstances and to quickly follow changing government regulations
- Robert Roshan (Interview 8) agrees with this and planning for a pandemic should be a permanent feature of risk committees.
- Margaret Harmer (Interview 9) emphasises risk management and checking your resources regularly.

However, on the other hand, Greg Quicke (Interview 14) is just rolling along. His business is doing well, and from the Authors' viewpoint he seems to be enjoying both the business and life in Broome.

VI. FAMILY BUSINESS

15. Are you in a family business and from your experience what do you think are the advantages and disadvantages of family working in the business?

A "family business" is a business where the actions of one or more families in the business determine the fate of the business. Most respondents were quite wary of the risks in working with family members. It does seem to work better where family members work in different areas which limits the potential for clashes.

- Margaret Harmer (Interview 9) noted that Compassionate Friends, the organisation she set up to assist bereaved parents, is a community family. So, this question perhaps does not relate. Alan Manly (Interview 11) and Greg Whateley (Interview 7) view UBSS is some ways similar to Margaret Harmer
- Greg Quicke (Interview 14) and Annemarie (Interview 13) both said their businesses are not family businesses, but they would not mind their children coming in.
- Art Phillips' (Interview 5) business is not a family business, although he assists his wife's business.
- Rahul Daga (Interview 2), Art Phillips (Interview 5), Matija Squire (Interview 10), and Jon Tse (Interview 12) say working with family and friends could work but only with setting careful ground rules and an understanding and sharing of responsibilities.
- Matija (Interview 10) says there are advantages as family members can share difficulties quite well, but each family business should be treated on a case-by-case basis.

- Jon Tse (Interview 12) says that the type and size of business may affect how well family business work, that is big business versus small start-ups have different dynamics.

Some of our respondents see the risk as too great. Sudhir Warrier (Interview 1), John Engelander (Interview 4) and Robert Roshan (Interview 8) belong to this view.

Some absolutely embrace family business: Himalee Karunasena (Interview 3), Alice and Philip (Interview 6) and James Barbour (Interview 15) are big supporters of family business.

It is clear that there are many different views on this issue, and it is well worth listening to their advice from a practical view.

Figure 54 - It is not easy running a business and raising a family at the same time

Summary Information

BACKGROUND TO INTERVIEWEE

No	Interviewee	Type of Entrepreneur	Business Lifecycle Stage at time of interview	The Interviewee's Technical qualification
1	Sudhir Warrier	Traditional Entrepreneur	Mature stage	Diploma Hotel Management
2	Rahul Daga	Technical Entrepreneur	Mature stage	Engineering qualification
3	Himalee Karunasena	Part time Entrepreneur	Mature stage	Accounting degree
4	John Engelander	Eco/Green Entrepreneur	Mature stage	Left school to work with his father (mentor)
5	Art Phillips	Part time Entrepreneur / Consultant	Mature stage	Left Julliard music school to play on the road
6	Alice Needham & Philip Chaplin	Serial/Mature Entrepreneur	Mature stage	Alice completed two years of university accounting. Philip completed a chef's apprenticeship. They left working in family businesses to work in one they both started.
7	Greg Whateley	Intrapreneur	Consultant/ Advisor	Qualifications in music, teaching and administration

Summary Information

No	Interviewee	Type of Entrepreneur	Business Lifecycle Stage at time of interview	The Interviewee's Technical qualification
8	Robert Roshan	Technical Entrepreneur	Mature stage	Studied Computer science and electronics
9	Margaret Harmer	Social entrepreneur	Consultant/ Advisor	Parents did not encourage university studies. Completed a business course and then became a secretary.
10	Matija Squire	Entrepreneur consultant	Consultant/ Advisor	As mature student did a double degree in arts and business
11	Alan Manly	Traditional / Unlikely / Accidental Entrepreneur	Mature stage	Electronics degree
12	Jon Tse	Innovative entrepreneur	Early stage	Accounting and law qualifications
13	Annemarie Manders	Agritourism Entrepreneur	Mature stage	Nursing qualifications
14	Greg Quicke	Life-style Entrepreneur	Mature stage	Left Uni to go diving
15	James Barbour	Young Start-up Entrepreneur	Mid stage	BA in Communications Studies. His minor study (Outdoor Education) was useful in the business and the foundation for his interpersonal communication skills and leadership ability.

Table 1 - Background to Interviewee

Note:

1. All of the above interviews are entrepreneurs, except Greg Whatley who is an intrapreneur. The main difference between the two is that an intrapreneur is an employee, and an entrepreneur is the founder who designs, launches, and manages a new business, which almost always starts out as a small business.
2. For discussion on the lifecycle, see Part C2, below.

SELECTED ANSWERS

No	Interviewee	What is Success	Set Routines	Family Business
1	Sudhir Warrier	Business results. Keeps personal issues separate	Yes	No
2	Rahul Daga	Results from hard work. Happy customers.	Yes	Yes
3	Himalee Karunasena	Happy family life, Financial independence, Helping those less fortunate than herself	Yes	Yes
4	John Engelander	Fulfilment from achievement and contributing	No	No
5	Art Phillips	Ability to follow one's passion	Yes	Not in his business (but he assists with his wife's business)
6	Alice Needham & Philip Chaplin	Ability to earn a living and have a few little wins	Yes	Yes
7	Greg Whateley	Earn a good income and provide quality outcomes	Yes	Staff treated like family members. But not a real "family business"
8	Robert Roshan	Strive to be the best version of yourself, enjoy the journey	Weekly not daily routine	No
9	Margaret Harmer	Meaningful life contribution	Not now, but yes at certain earlier times of her life	A community type family. But not a real "family business"

No	Interviewee	What is Success	Set Routines	Family Business
10	Matija Squire	Alignment of work to her values and achieving belonging with family and community	No	No
11	Alan Manly	Well provided for family and security – see "The Castle" movie	Yes	At times. Wife and daughter.
12	Jon Tse	Varies depends on stages. Currently chasing sales growth	Partly	No
13	Annmarie Manders	Creating something that is accepted and recognised	Yes	No
14	Greg Quicke	Contribute to humanity	Only when doing shows	No
15	James Barbour	Happy smiling customers with his product	Yes	Yes. He owns the business, but his wife works in it.

Table 2 - Selected Answers

Part C:

The Theory

In this part there are eight sections:

- C1 What is an Entrepreneur?
- C2 Entrepreneurial Business Lifecycle
- C3 The Entrepreneur's Lifecycle
- C4 Entrepreneurship is not for everyone!
- C5 Do you have to be smart to be an Entrepreneur?
- C6 Reasons for business failure
- C7 Sources of finance
- C8 Final reflections

What is an Entrepreneur?

"But as an entrepreneur, you have to feel like you can jump out of an aeroplane because you're confident that you'll catch a bird flying by. It's an act of stupidity, and most entrepreneurs go play because the bird doesn't come by, but a few times it does."

Reed Hastings , CEO Netflix

OVERVIEW

As we have already seen in the Introduction to this book entrepreneurship is the creation or extraction of value, accepting risks beyond what is normally encountered in starting a business, and receiving rewards other than simply economic ones.

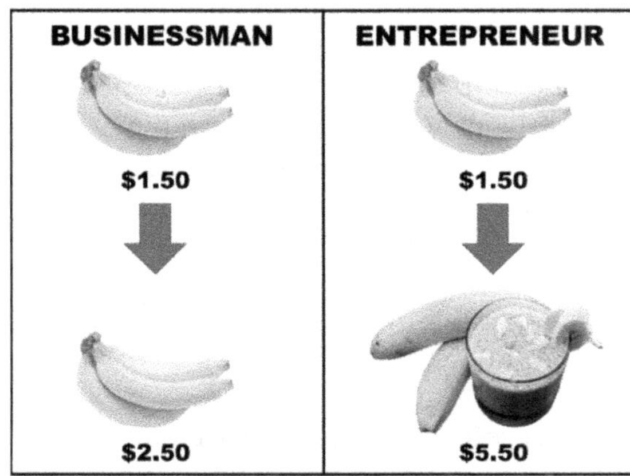

Figure 55 - Businessman vs Entrepreneur

The simple image at left clearly shows the difference between a business person and an entrepreneur.

- The *business person* often only buys themselves a job (and works longer, and harder under more stress to earn their salary than when they worked for someone else).
- However, the *entrepreneur* earns a salary AND makes a profit on top of that. They do this by adding value.

CONCERNS

The entrepreneur is concerned about:

- the creation or extraction of value generally [note that entrepreneurship is a process of creating or innovating something new of value by devoting the necessary time and effort]
- the risk beyond what is normally encountered in starting a business. [note that this occurs by accepting and acknowledging the necessary financial, psychological, and social risks]
- values other than simply economic ones [note that this relates to receiving both monetary and personal satisfaction rewards and the freedom to do what you want.]

WHAT ARE THE DIFFERENT TYPES OF ENTREPRENEURS?

"All humans are entrepreneurs not because they should start companies but because the will to create is encoded in human DNA."

Reid Hoffman, co-founder LinkedIn

We found that the available literature on the various categories of Entrepreneur to vary extremely widely. A quick look on the Internet will give you lots of options ranging from 3,4,5,7,8 to 20 varieties. Below are two examples of what we found in the literature:

Example 1: 4 types

- Small business – this represents the majority of small businesses, for example a café
- Scalable start-up – less common. They have a new idea to be developed, for example high tech

- Large Company – Often Intrapreneurs working within a large company to expand business. An example is Greg Whateley.
- Social Entrepreneur – Willing to take on risk to tackle a community issue. An example is Margaret Harmer (Interview 9).

Source: https://onlinebusiness.northeastern.edu/blog/types-of-entrepreneurship/ (viewed 8 October 2021)

Example 2: 10 types

- Buyer – Previously successful Entrepreneurs looking for a good buy. For example, Alan Manly.
- Hustler – People that dream big and using networking to sometimes "make it". For example, Donald Trump.
- Imitator – Willing to build a business around existing idea. For example, Mark Zuckerberg (Facebook) and Robert Roshan (Interview 8).
- Innovator – Go-getters desperate to build a legacy. For example, Larry Page (Alphabet)
- Financier – Wealthy individuals using personal brand to get into ventures (Paris Hilton)
- Prodigy -Highly intelligent, often have little business training. For example, Steve Jobs (Apple)
- Researcher – Careful analysts to ensure a fool proof venture. For example, Larry Ellison (oracle)
- Short -Timer- Mix of above but looking to get and out for a profit. For example, Brian Acton (Whats-app)
- Solopreneur – Want to do everything themselves. For example, Neil Patel digital marketing expert

Source: https://www.bondcollective.com/blog/types-of-entrepreneurs/ (viewed 8 October 2021)

EVERYONE IS UNIQUE

When we look at each of our interviewees, we realised that everyone was unique and had their own style. It is often difficult to generalise. Nevertheless, we have attempted to categorise our interviewees with a combination of existing categories and our own. Categorising is useful as it assists us to show the different ways people can get into entrepreneurship.

THE "UNLIKELY ENTREPRENEUR"

We were very taken by the "Unlikely Entrepreneur", people that had no intention of taking risks to build something but somehow accidentally fell into entrepreneurship. Several of our interviewees fell into this category including Margaret Harmer (Interview 9) and UBSS founder, and CEO, Alan Manly (Interview 11). Indeed, he wrote an autobiographical book called *"The Unlikely Entrepreneur"* See Manly (2020) for references.

The Entrepreneurial Business Lifecycle

Below is one example of the lifecycle of a business (and in C.3 we will cover the lifecycle of the entrepreneur):

Stage 1 - Develop the business concept
Plan launch
Obtain the resources
(see UBSS Book 1: "Part 1 - Starting the Business")

Stage 2 – Growth Phase
Create and modify as needed.
Make quick changes to establish the business.
(see UBSS Book 1: "Part 2: Operating the Business")

Stage 3 – Stabilise or Exit stage
Working on business for long term sustainability
Alternative is to look at exiting.
(see UBSS Book 1: "Part 3 – Ending the Business").

Stage 4 – Leveraging on all the knowledge and experience.
Ability to give back
Contribute the next generation

Figure 56 - The Entrepreneurial Business Lifecycle (Source: Jankoff and Bendel)

Note:

1. Often this cycle is represented by a graph that starts low, rises and then either continues to rise or drops as in a normal distribution curve. For an example see the next Figure.

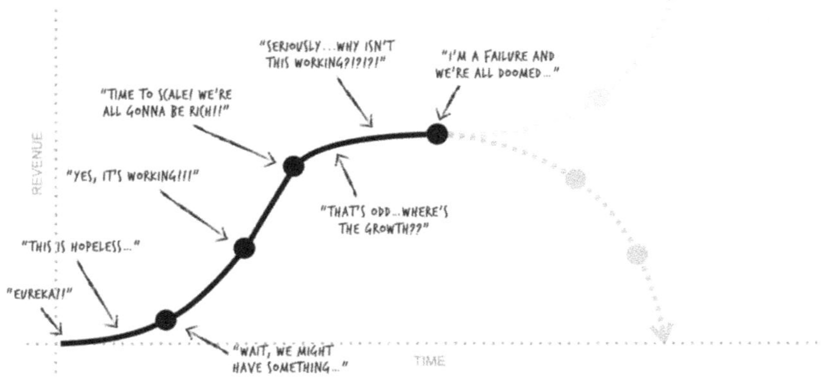

Figure 57 - An Example of a Business at the crossroads in the Lifecycle (Source: https://scalable.co/library/entrepreneurial-lifecycle/)

Note:

1. There are a number of stages in the typical lifecyle of a new venture. For example, according to Frederick (2018) the life cycle stages are the stages through which a venture progresses, include new venture development, start-up, growth, stabilisation and innovation or decline.
2. See Scalable (2021) for an interesting story about a business failure which the CEO did not see coming, and when it became apparent, he did not know what to do about it. It is entitled, "The entrepreneurial lifecycle and what I learned from nearly bankrupting my first company".

The Entrepreneur's Lifecycle

In Section C2 we considered the lifecycle of the business and now we will consider the lifecycle of the entrepreneur, that is the owner(s). The difference is that here the focus is on the person rather than the business.

As you can see from the below Figure, the entrepreneur goes through a less uniform process. For example, just as a builder looks back at the houses constructed, entrepreneurs similarly seek to review what they have created and enjoy the process of keeping doing and hopefully improving on the model. If they can earn extra profit on top of a good income, then that is a real bonus. Entrepreneurs come in all shapes and sizes, ages, races and religions. They can be young or old, they can exit early or late. It all depends on the individual, and their surrounding circumstances.

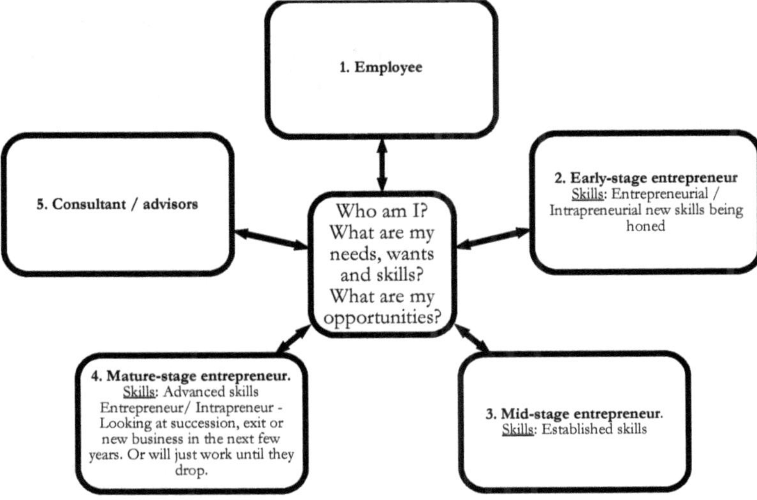

Figure 58 - The Entrepreneur's Lifecycle (Source: Jankoff and Bendel)

The process can be circular, and entrepreneurs come in and out at any stage of the process. They often start as an employee and then move into entrepreneurship (as we saw with Warrier (Interview 1), Rahul (Interview 2), John Englander (Interview 4). Himalee (Interview 3) stayed as an employee 9 to 5 on weekdays, and after-hours she worked as an entrepreneur.

Let us now consider an example. Take an employee who starts a venture and then exits and comes back as an employee (for fuller details see the Bob Greengrass case study in Section 1.3.1 of the authors' first UBSS book (Jankoff and Bendel, 2020), Business War Stories from the Trenches". Initially he was an employee, then went into business which didn't work so went returned as an employee. He did this because he wanted more control of his work, so he went back into business then that didn't work so went back to being an employee).

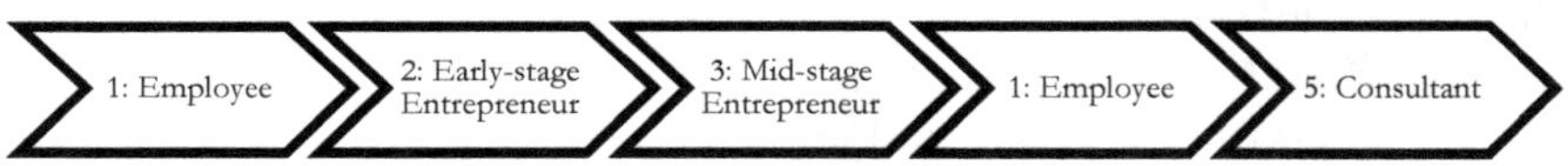

Figure 59 - Bob Greengrass's Entrepreneurial Business Lifecycle (Source: Jankoff and Bendel)

Note:

1. The numbers refer to the Figure 58 lifecycle stages
2. After all his experiences, Bob may wish to advise on his experiences and work as consultant, that is work in Lifecycle Stage 5.

Entrepreneurship is not for everyone!

It probably goes without saying but taking entrepreneurial risks on is not for everyone. The stress and long hours that are needed is enough to put many people off. It is hard to stay positive with the inevitable setbacks and failures. If it was that easy everyone would be an entrepreneur. In the authors' first UBSS book (Jankoff and Bendel, 2020) the authors explored in more detail who and how people can evaluate the choice of business and the resources required to make a go of it. See Part 1, Starting the Business.

One of the authors usually said the following when he was asked about whether the client should go into business on their own. He said "if you start your own business, you will be working twice as long, twice as hard, with twice as much stress with half the pay and probably twice the enjoyment that you were getting from your job. If you're willing to accept that, then you should consider working in your own business."

The author knew a case of a person who had been an employee for their whole life and then late in life bought into the ownership of the company. He was unable to change his mindset, generally preferred the status quo, was unwilling to make some difficult decisions where work was involved and unprepared to put the extra time in when needed. He nearly ruined the business.

Entrepreneurship is not for everyone!

Do you have to be smart to be an Entrepreneur?

When analysing successful entrepreneurs it became clear how important people skills were compared to raw intelligence. People skills, also known as "Emotional intelligence" or "Human relations skills" seem to be key. These people understand that you can buy or hire skills needed to provide the intelligence. The real skill is therefore to hire people smarter than they are and manage them productively. If you are smart enough to understand this point then you are smart enough to be an entrepreneur, although that is only the start of what is needed. You need to be well organised. See the quotations at the end of Matija's interview (Interview 10).

Daniel Goleman, who pioneered Emotional Intelligence (EI) discusses EI in his Emotional Intelligence YouTube video (Goleman, 2021). He suggests that in order to effectively run a business one really needs both IQ and EQ, that is intelligence and emotional intelligence

When one of the authors worked for an accounting firm very early in his career and was requested to look after one of the wealthy clients. The client was a successful jeweller with a chain of stores. He was "old school" looking after his money carefully and did not drive flashy cars or flaunt his wealth. He lived close to the author so he would regularly drop in to the author about updating his accounts and would talk and have coffee. The author was very interested to see what made a successful businessman tick. The businessman was not particularly intelligent. The author couldn't understand how the jeweller became so successful. One day the author asked his employer's senior partner about this. The senior partner said, "you clearly don't understand the essential elements of success. The jeweller has street smarts, he knows how to buy good quality merchandise at very cheap prices. That's it! The rest is just hiring good management and being prepared to take calculated risks."

Reasons for business failure

OVERVIEW

In the authors' first book for UBSS entitled "Business War Stories from the Trenches" (Jankoff and Bendel, 2020) we stated under Reasons for failure (see Chapter 1, Section 1.2.11);

> **Reasons for failure**
>
> According to the U.S. Small Business Administration, over 50% of small businesses fail in the first year and 95% fail within the first five years. Other studies around the world have similar results. Different research says different things, but the common answer is, regardless of the industry, failure (especially in the early years) is the result of lack of management experience and insufficient money when needed.

What we see from the above is that most business failures occur in the first few years after commencement and as time goes the likelihood of failure reduces. Research shows that the likelihood of failure is reduced when one undertakes business management training.

THE TWO KEY REASONS FOR BUSINESS FAILURE

In summary, the two key reasons for business failure are lack of management experience and insufficient money when needed. We will now discuss each in turn.

FAILURE REASON NO 1: LACK OF MANAGEMENT EXPERIENCE

The purpose of this book is to explore the "management" by interviewing entrepreneurs. Hopefully reading through the cases the reader will gain some real-life insights into the various management styles and techniques.

Some principles of management are enduring, but managers need to be continually adapting to changing times. Each facet of the framework—from planning, to organising, to leading, to controlling—has to be adapted to take advantage of, and to manage in, our changing world. Global trends affect both the style and the substance of management. As the world becomes more global, managers find themselves leading workforces that may be distributed across the country—and the world. Workers are more educated, but more is expected of them.

The realm of managers is expanding. As a leader, managers will be a role model in the organisation, setting the tone not just for what gets done but how it gets done. Increasingly, good business practice extends to stewardship, not just of the organisation but of the environment and community at large. Ethics and values-based leadership aren't just good ideas—they're vital to attracting talent and retaining loyal customers and business partners.

Over a century ago Henri Fayol came up with which now called the planning-organising-leading-controlling (POLC) management framework. Fayol is widely acknowledged as a founder of modern management methods. The POLC framework is summarised in the following figure.

Planning	**Organising**	**Leading**	**Controlling**
1. vision and mission	1. organisational design	1. leadership	1. systems / processors
2. strategizing	2. culture	2. decision making	2. strategic human resource is
3. goals and objectives	3. social networks	3. communications	
		4. groups / teams	
		5. motivation	

Table 3 - The POLC Framework (Source: Saylordot - 2021)

Businesses are frequently not run in a business-like manner.

To the detriment of the business

Figure 60 - Running a business

FAILURE REASON NO 2: LACK OF FINANCE

A business ignores attention to ensuring sufficient financial resources at its peril. Finance has not been a central part of our interviews, but it permeates the interviews (and our first book as well) and as we have seen it is the second critical element in a successful business. Financial issues are discussed in greater detail below.

Sources of finance

THE TYPICAL WAY TO FINANCE A SMALL BUSINESS

Small business tends to start by "maxing out" their credit cards, mortgaging their home if possible, and family and friends (and fools) assisting. When that is all used up, they either get more money from wherever they can or let the business collapse. So, what then are the various ways to finance the set up and operating a business?

THE CIRCULAR MOVEMENT OF CASH

It is vital for a business person to understand how the circular movement of cash works. For a diagrammatical representation see the figure below. In order to run a business, there needs to be money, and the source of this money is Step 1. The money raised then goes into the bucket of cash and it is used to procure goods and services (Step 2), then used to operate the business (Step 3) and then to make sales (Step 4). The money comes back in again as sales proceeds.

Unfortunately, there are leakages at all of the four steps. For example, money is borrowed at a very high rate of interest, or you have to give away part of ownership of your business. When procuring you might buy ten items but only eight work. In the operations phase some of your employees may not be contributing as they are "sleeping" on the job (see image below). In the sales phase you may sell 10 items but only get paid for eight, or they take a long time to get paid.

A non-contributing employee is not good for the organisation.

Figure 61 - Employee contribution

In the figure below you will see the clockwise circular movement of cash, which includes the four different steps. Below the figure we discuss the two different sources of funds: the internal source and the external source.

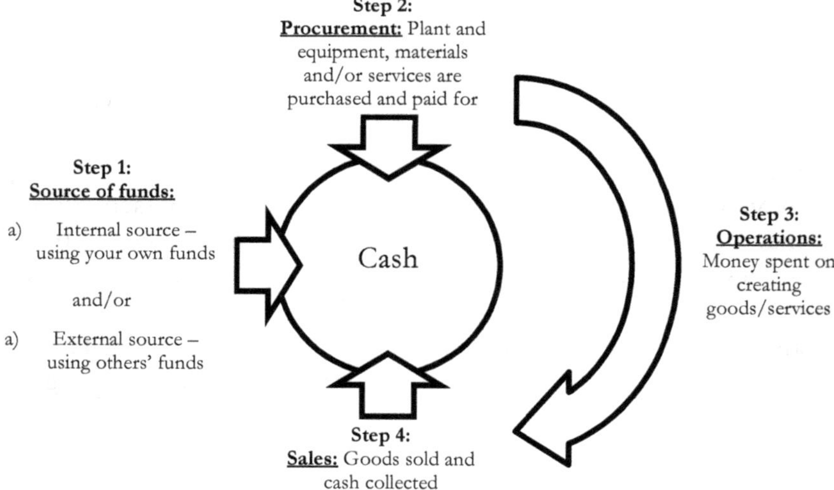

Figure 62 - The Circular Movement of Cash (Source: Jankoff - 2021)

Note: Funding and finance are commonly terms used interchangeability although slightly different technical meanings. Funding is actually the money provided by companies or by a government sector for a specific purpose, whereas financing is a process of receiving capital or money for business purpose, and it is usually provided by financial institutions, such as, banks or other lending agencies.

THE FIRST SOURCE OF FUNDS – INTERNAL

This is where the organisation uses its *own* funds:

- Cash: in bank
- Assts: sell them
- Other: For example, Bootstrapping (taking on a second job).

THE SECOND SOURCE OF FUNDS – EXTERNAL

Using *others'* funds:

- Debt: Cash borrowed
- Equity: Selling a part of the business. This includes crowd sourced equity funding (CSF). See below for an elaboration.
- Gifts (from friends, family and fools)
- Grants (from government, societies etc.)

CROWD SOURCED EQUITY FUNDING (CSF).

As this is not a textbook on finance, we will not discuss details of each of the different above sources of finance, including their advantages and disadvantages as they can be easily located through the internet. However, we do quickly wish to discuss crowdsourced equity funding (CSF) because this is new to Australia, and it may assist the reader. CSF was introduced to Australia on 29 September

2017 and is regulated by the Australian Securities and Investment Commission (ASIC).

CSF was introduced to meet a gap in the market for very small businesses to access finance as a result of the major banks becoming more risk averse. Crowd-sourced funding is different from the donation or reward-based crowdfunding. In CSF, eligible start-ups and small and medium-sized businesses can raise money from the public to start or grow their business or pay off debts. People who contribute money can invest up to $10,000 in exchange for shares in the business. It generally is not easy for the investors to get their capital back again, although there are moves to create a platform to facilitate trading. For further information see ASIC (2021). One of the first and largest licensed Equity crowdfunding platforms is Birchal. See Birchall (2021).

Final reflections

INTRODUCTION

The process of talking to our everyday entrepreneurs has been illuminating on the nature of being successful in a competitive business world with some surprising results including the focus on non-monetary rewards and fairly modest ambitions for monetary rewards. They were all optimistic about the opportunities surrounding them, and indeed all of us. A few interesting points arose from our discussions:

ADVISERS

Advisers have an important place, but the decisions are ultimately made by those with "skin in the game", that is, those most affected which usually is the owner(s). If everyone slavishly listened to their professional business advisers' warnings before they went into business, most businesses would never start! Warrier (Interview 1) is a good example where one venture did not work with advice, and one worked well without advice. Alice and Philip (Interview 6) did extensive business plans on a food wrap business that ultimately did not work due to high competition, but they opened their dog treat business on gut feel and it turned out to be successful. We feel that getting professional advice and planning are vital, as is "gut-feel", but the latter often comes from long experience and going through the planning processes first. The term "Gut-feel" arose out of discussions in Question 9, which related to providing a case that did not go well and why. Each of the 15 interviewees were asked the same question.

IMPLEMENTATION/ COMMERCIALISATION

There are plenty of "ideas" people, but it is the implementation and commercialisation that most people find difficult and where business failure is common. So not only do we need good ideas, but we need ways to implement and commercialise them. Our Entrepreneurs all understood this point very well and perhaps this is one of the major differences between employee and entrepreneurs.

According to Investopedia commercialisation is the process of bringing new products or services to market. The broader act of commercialisation entails production, distribution, marketing, sales, customer support, and other key functions critical to achieving the commercial success of the new product or service. See Investopedia (2021c).

WHAT DETERMINES SUCCESS?

Most statistical assumptions about people's performance revolve around the Bell curve (also known as Normal Distribution). It is used in a wide variety of applications including academic grading. Research states that whilst it is easy to understand, it is often not reflected in the real world. See below for a look at the distribution of people's performance.

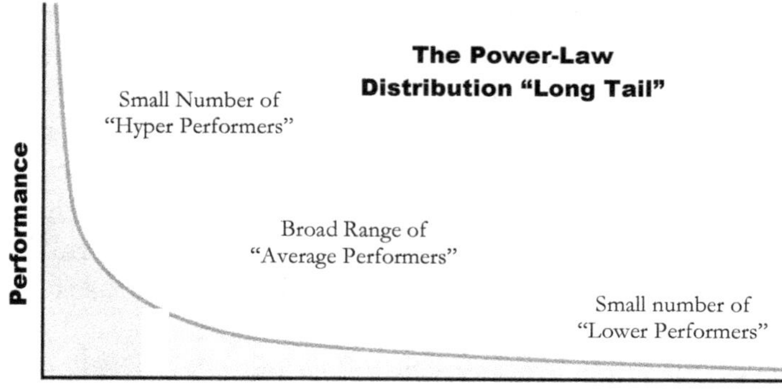

Figure 63 - The Myth Of The Bell Curve: Look For The Hyper-Performers (Source: Forbes – 2021)

The shaded part of the left of the above image indicates that there are a few hyper-performers which stand out. Bill Gates says that without a few of these people Microsoft wouldn't exist. For example, ask yourself would the Premiers of the National Rugby League (NRL) or the Australian Football League (AFL) have won without their top two or three elite champions?

The shaded part on the right-hand side of the above graph also shows that the majority of us are just "average performers". This is good news as regardless of intelligence or skills, most of us can achieve a great deal depending on our motivation. We have already spoken about the need for EQ, also known as EI (Emotional Intelligence) see Part C.5, "Do you have to be smart to be an Entrepreneur?" Another important factor is that organisations, including football teams, need a team of performers to back up and support their stars, even if they are only "average".

Remember **Steve Jobs'** quotation on teamwork: *"Great things in business are never done by one person; they're done by a team of people."* As we said above ideas and their implementation are both vital.

Authors' note: good news for us

Part D:

References, Figures, Index etc

In this part there are four sections:

- D1 Compilation of References
- D2 List of figures
- D3 List of tables
- D4 Index

Compilation of References

Reference
ASIC (2021). *https://asic.gov.au/regulatory-resources/financial-services/crowd-sourced-funding/* Viewed 29 October 2021.
Birchall (2021): *https://www.birchal.com/* Viewed 29 October 2021.
Bond Collective (2021). What is a lifestyle entrepreneur and how to become one? *https://www.bondcollective.com/blog/lifestyle-entrepreneur/* Viewed 29 October 2021.
Calcium Carbonate Org (2021). 10 Things you might not know about CaCO3 (Calcium carbonate) *http://www.calcium-carbonate.org.uk/calcium-carbonate/caco3-10facts.asp* Viewed 29 October 2021.
Cleaning Hack (2021). 9 Interesting Historical Facts About the Vacuum Cleaner. https://cleaning-hacks.sharkclean.co.uk/9-interesting-historical-facts-about-the-vacuum-cleaner/. Viewed 29 October 2021.
Enicbdmed (2021). Eco-entrepreneurship: do you know what it is? *https://www.enicbcmed.eu/resmyle-eco-entrepreneurship-do-you-know-what-it* Viewed 29 October 2021.
Forbes (2021). The Myth Of The Bell Curve: Look For The Hyper-Performers. *https://www.forbes.com/sites/joshbersin/2014/02/19/the-myth-of-the-bell-curve-look-for-the-hyper-performers/?sh=fcf2f36bca01* Viewed 29 October 2021).
Frederick, H., O'Connor, A., Kuratko, D. F. (2018). Entrepreneurship, 5th Edition, Cengage South Melbourne).
Goleman, D. (2021). Emotional Intelligence. 3 minute 32 second video. *http://www.youtube.com/watch?v=wJhfKYzKc0s* Viewed 29 October 2021.

Reference
Growdirect (2021). Fun Facts about Lavender. *https://www.growerdirect.com/fun-facts-about-lavender* Viewed 29 October 2021.
Imgur (2021). When everyone is upvoting Austin Powers but you're just trying to get a dog adopted. *https://imgur.com/gallery/O350MUI* Viewed 7 November 2021.
Inc.com (2021) Research ranks Australia 8th in world for proportion of women entrepreneurs. *https://womensagenda.com.au/business/research-ranks-australia-8th-in-world-for-women-entrepreneurs/* Viewed 29 October 2021
Instantprint (2021). 11 Common Phrases and Sayings That Actually Originated in the Printing Industry. *https://www.instantprint.co.uk/printspiration/be-inspired/everyday-phrases-you-didn%E2%80%99t-realise-originated-from-print* Viewed 29 October 2021
Investopedia (2021a). What is an entrepreneur? *https://www.investopedia.com/terms/e/entrepreneur.asp* Viewed 29 October 2021
Investopedia (2021b). What Is a Social Entrepreneur? *https://www.investopedia.com/terms/s/social-entrepreneur.asp* Viewed 29 October 2021
Investopedia (2021c). Commercialization. *https://www.investopedia.com/terms/c/commercialization.asp* Viewed 29 October 2021
Jankoff (2021). Manage Your Contracts (5th Ed). Melbourne: Business Education and Consulting Pty Ltd, Melbourne.
Jankoff, C. and Bendel, D. (2020). Business War Stories from the Trenches, UBSS, Sydney.
Manly (2020). For references see *https://www.alanmanly.com.au/the-unlikely-entrepreneur* Viewed 10 October 2021. To read about more "unlikely entrepreneurs" see *https://www.shoppingcartelite.com/articles/4-improbable-success-stories-of-unlikely-entrepren* Viewed 29 October 2021.
Mobile-Cuisine (2021). Pickle Fun Facts. *https://mobile-cuisine.com/did-you-know/pickle-fun-facts/* Viewed 29 October 2021
National Ag Law Centre (2021). Agritourism – An Overview. *https://nationalaglawcenter.org/overview/agritourism/* Viewed 29 October 2021

Reference
Newsweek (2021). 30 Fascinating Facts About Wine That You Never Knew. *https://www.newsweek.com/amplify/30-fascinating-facts-about-wine-that-you-never-knew*
Popular Mechanics (2021). Prediction 1937: Microwave Cooking. *https://www.popularmechanics.com/flight/g462/future-that-never-was-next-gen-tech-concepts/* Viewed 29 October 2021
Reader's Digest (2021). 12 Historical Predictions That Completely, Utterly Missed the Mark. *https://www.readersdigest.ca/culture/worst-predictions/* Viewed 29 October 2021
Sam USACE Army (2021). A History of Steamboats. *https://www.sam.usace.army.mil/Portals/46/docs/recreation/OP-CO/montgomery/pdfs/10thand11th/ahistoryofsteamboats.pdf*Viewed 29 October 2021
Saylordot (2021). History, Globalization, and Values-Based Leadership. *https://saylordotorg.github.io/text_principles-of-management-v1.1/s07-00-history-globalization-and-valu.html*Viewed 29 October 2021
Scalable (2021). The entrepreneurial lifecycle and what I learned from nearly bankrupting my first company. *https://scalable.co/library/entrepreneurial-lifecycle/* Viewed 29-10-21
Sheet Music Plus (2021). Top 10 Facts About the Guitar. *https://blog.sheetmusicplus.com/2018/02/21/top-10-facts-about-the-guitar/* Viewed 29 October 2021
The balance small business (2021) How to Start a Side Hustle While Keeping Your Day Job. *https://www.thebalancesmb.com/how-to-start-a-side-business-while-keeping-your-day-job-4115403* Viewed 29 October 2021

List of Figures

List of Tables

Index

Notes pages

www.ingramcontent.com/pod-product-compliance
Lightning Source LLC
Chambersburg PA
CBHW050523190326
41458CB00005B/1642

* 9 7 8 1 9 0 7 4 5 3 3 2 8 *